James Barker

The Royal Robe

James Barker

The Royal Robe

ISBN/EAN: 9783337225810

Printed in Europe, USA, Canada, Australia, Japan

Cover: Foto ©Thomas Meinert / pixelio.de

More available books at **www.hansebooks.com**

THE
ROYAL ROBE:
OR, A
TREATISE
OF
Meeknesse.

Upon Col. 3. 12.
Wholly tending to
PEACEABLENESSE.

By *James Barker*

BEATI PACIFICI. Matth. 5.9.

The Meek shall inherit the earth, and shall delight themselves in the abundance of peace. Psal. 37. 11.

Tranquillus Deus, tranquillat omnia. *S. Bern. super. Cant. Serm.* 23. p. 631. Col. 1.

LONDON, Printed by *E. M.* for *Robert Gibbs*, at the golden-Ball in *Chancery*-lane. 1661.

To the Honorable
Sr *HARBOTLE GRIMSTON*
BARONET,
SPEAKER of the Houſe of
C O M M O N S.

SIR,

Ere mine *abilities* as large as my *Will*, 8r could I perform what might chal-lenge the *Applauſe* of all good men, All this from me is a *debt* to your *Merit*. What *obligations* of duty and thankfulneſſe you have laid upon me, I every where find : what *Acknow•*

A   *ledge-*

ledgemenrs I fhall mak, I am
ftill to feek: but in the want
of better, I humbly offer this
Treatife of Meekneffe: unworthy
(I confeffe) your *judgment* or
acceptance : yet doubt not you
will give it entertainment for
the *fubjects* fake:for in my hear-
ing (from his mouth by whom
the *Commons of England* fpeak
unto the *King*) *Meeknes* hath receiv'd the comendation of an
excellent *fubject*. *Meeknefs* is a-
nother thing than it is comon-
ly taken to be, well known to
you, which makes you fo *eminent* in the practice of it.

And your *difcreet zeal* doth
fpeak your *courage*, no leffe,
than your *Chriftian meeknefs*,

your *Wisdome* (special qualifications in a *Magistrate*): which seconded with your great *experience*, and *Piety*; who more likely (considering the place you sustain)to do *God*, the *King*, the *Church*, and his *Countrey* better service.

Sir, I send forth *this Book* to you, with the same blessing that *Israel* sent forth his sons unto *Joseph* (*God Almighty give thee mercy in the sight of the man*)the Author and the Work do need the *Patronage* of a person of note and eminencie, both for *Goodness* & *Power*; such an one as your *self* is:from whom they may receive *countenance & pro-*

A 3   *tecti-*

tection. In this what I have perform'd, I humbly submit to your *Grave Censure*, being confident you will not deny it a favourable perusal ; in it I *complain* not of *Wrongs* , for *complaints* are not pleasing where they are necessary, my *project* only is to commend Meekness.

This *Treatise* of Meekness I have entituled (THE ROYAL ROBE) not only because the *Apostle* proposes it as a *Garment* to be put on; and *Synesius* tells me; *Clemency* or Meekness is (βασιλικώ'τατον) a vertue meet for a *Prince :* but also because his sacred Majesty our Soveraigne Lord the *King* (amongst other

A 3   Prince-

Princely and Heroick vertues that beautifie his *Royal person*) hath fulfill'd the *Apostles rule*, in *Putting on* Meekness, which as a ROYAL ROBE he wears, and appears conspicuous, illustrious and exemplary in it in the eys of al his people. *Clemency* or Meekness hath in it a *majesty* aswel as *sweetness*: a Clement Prince is an object for love and wonder to stand amazed at; unto whom all men (*tanquam ad clarum ac beneficum sidus certatim advolant.*) The *Orator* praising *Cæsar* above all commends him for his *Clemencie*, that his *fortune* had nothing greater than that he had *power*, his *nature* nothing

better

better than that he had *will* to
save many; and what greater
honor can there be, than to be,
what *Titus Veſpaſian* is ſaid to
be (*Deliciæ humani Generis*)the
Darling of the World. And
now if the World be compos'd
to follow their *Rulers* (*Regis
ad exemplum totus componitur orbis*) and the diſpoſition of our
Nation do incline them to *Imitation* (apt to follow the faſhion) there is great hopes that
Meekneſs will come into *faſhion*
(being thus commended, by the
Apoſtles *Rule*; the Kings *Example*; the practice of ſuch *Wor-
thies* as your ſelf; with the wholſome *leſsons* of pious *Paſtors*)
and

and that such (who were as ravening *Wolves* scattering the
flock, and devouring one another : frighting the *Shepherds*
(the *Magistrates* aswel as Mi-
nisters) from their *Charge*,
wrought upon, and won by
these means,)will be converted, and become *new men* : will
follow after Meeknes, and approve themselves the Lambs
of *Christs flock*, harmlesse, gentle, meek, quiet and peaceable,
then shall we live to see good
dayes; *Jerusalem* in prosperity
all our life long, and peace upon *Israel*.

And the *God of heaven* who
hath made you *honourable*, and
placed

placed you in the *eye of the Land*, a *Patron* of *learning*, a fin-cere *friend* of *Religion*, an *encourager* of *vertue*, encrease in you his *graces*, direct you in your *courses*, profper you in your honorable *undertakings*, fill you full of *dayes* and *bleffings*, and at laft bring you to his *everlafting Kingdom*, which is, and fhall be the prayer of

Your Honours in all faith-

ful and humble obfervance

Auguft 7.
1660.

James Barker.

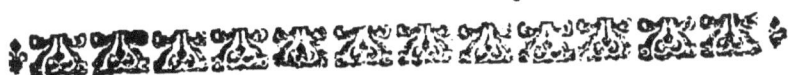

The Epistle Dedicatory.

And truly Madam, *I cannot but let you know, what* satisfaction *it is to me, that my* Meditations *were directed to a subject* so suitable *to the quiet temper of your Religious mind:* so agreeable *to the constant practice of your vertuous life,* meek and peaceable.

It is your Meeknesse, *Madam, that gives a lustre to all your other* vertues *and* Graces, *which beautifie your person, and Christian conversation, and render you an* Ornament *to your* Sex: *no plaiting of* ~~the~~ Hair, *wearing of* Gold, *putting on of* Apparel, *do set forth a* Lady, *in that high estimation with* God *and good men, as her exemplary* vertues *do; those outward* Adornings *you do not use them; for you do not need them;* God *having abundantly stored you, out of his own* Treasury *of nature and* Grace.

Good Madam, *I know it is unpleasing to you, to read your own* Commendation *(though never so well deserv'd) yet I beseech you give me leave to acknowledge to the* Glory of God, *what I have observ'd to the* joy of my heart: *and when* you *shall be taken into* heaven; *and I shall be turned into* dust, *let this be written for a* memorial *to the world; of your* Merit, *and my* duty.

In

The Epistle Dedicatory.

In Treating of Meeknesse, *I am not ignorant that* (Lúpum auribus teneo) Anger *the one extreme is a hot, heady, fierce and fiery passion* (like a wild beast) Meeknesse *is the* Mean *that tames it.* And so! *here through* Meeknesse *I have* (with some industry) beaten a plain path for the sober moderate Christian *to walk in.*

And now were it not to trespasse too farre upon a noble patience, *I could give in a* Breviat *of my* Book: *but I presume of a candid interpretation from your* Ladiship, (*if in a very few words*) *I humbly offer an* Assay *of what I have treated on.*

May it please your Ladiship *then! I have endeavoured to settle the weak and wavering mind: to quiet the wilful and unruly spirit: to set the heart in a right frame and temper both towards* God, *and also towards man: to suppresse impatience, murmuring, fretting and repining: to shew how sufferings are to be entertain'd, and afflictions of what kind soever undergone, with* a patient and quiet mind.

I have set forth Meeknesse *as a most rare vertue: and such that brings beauty, safety, dignity to them that have it: and not only fils the soul and concience with* tranquillity *and serenity: but doth fashion the countenance, carriage, language and out-*
ward

The Epistle Dedicatory.

ward comportment to amiablenesse *and sweetnesse It doth pass by* indignities, *puts up* injuries, *bear.* Reproaches, *and forbears* Revenge, *qualifies the heat of* passions, *rectifies the disorder of* Affections, *appeases* Distractions, *heals* Distempers, *reconciles* differences *both in judgment and practice. Here is propounded also a* means *for the stopping of private* quar-rels: *a* way *opened to* publick peace: *directions given for the ordering of our* Civil *and* Christian conversation : *and certain* Instructions *about order and* Decency *in the publick duties of* Religion ; *setting down* the nature *and* use *of things* indifferent, *and how* Christian liberty *is to be regulated to* peaceablenesse.

And this I shall ever reckon amongst the chiefest blessings of my holy Calling, *to be in any measure* Instrumental *in promoting the* publick peace: *and by the* Grace of God (*so long as I live*) *next to the* Truth of Christ, *the* peace of the Church, *shall be the* Center *both of my studies and practice.*

And seeing by the Providence of God, *and by the great* Wisdom, *and unwearied* pains *of our* Rulers, *we have attain'd to that* happinesse, *which of late years we could rather wish, than* hope *for: and seeing above* hope , *and beyond* expectation,

God

The Epistle Dedicatory.

God hath appear'd *for our* salvation *and* settlement *both in* Church *and* Common-wealth; *it were to be lamented that any should be found so great an enemy to their own* felicity, *as to call for* new troubles, *when the wounds of the* old *(though healed with a tender and skilful hand) are yet* blew: *or so far in love with their own* misery, *as to put away from them this precious* mercy, *and not rather with heart and both hands to entertain it, to be contented and thankful.*

Most honoured Lady, *God hath given* you *your hearts desire, to live in* peace *under a* rightful Government. *And the* Affections *of your most worthy* husband *and* your self *so happily meeting in the* love *of* Truth *and* Peace : *in the dislike of* Error *and* Schism : *your continual practice of* Piety, *and in the* worship *and* service *of God your chearful* conformity *(to the Order of the* Church of England *by* Law *established) doth let the world know the most truly* Religious, *and most* judicious, *are most* conformable. *Long may you both live, (to move like* stars, *in your own* Sphere *) a light and direction in every* good way, *to all that are below you.* Ile adde no more; *after I have beg'd of your* Ladiship *to accept of this my most* humble service ; *and of my most* hearty wishes, *for a happy* New-year.

And I pray God, every Revolution *of the* year, *may bring with it a* Renovation *of your* health, honour, *and outward* prosperity, *with an encrease of all spiritual* Graces, *and heavenly* blessings, *until you come to the exchange of time for* Eternity, *for the which I shall not cease to be importunate at the* Throne *of* Grace *whilst I am*

Jan. 2. 1660.   R. A. D. V. E. R.

THE
ROYAL ROBE:
OR, A
TREATISE
OF
MEEKNESSE.

COL. 3. 12.

Put on ——— Meeknesse.

THere is mention in Scripture of a *first*, and *secoud Adam*; the *first* is of the earth, earthly : the *second* is the *Lord* from *heaven*. These *two* are the *two principles* of *mankind* distinguish'd in-

1 Cor. 15. 47.
Nam ut ille fuit humani generis princeps, secundum carnalem

B   to

to a twofold eſtate of *Nature* and *Grace.* The *firſt Adam* is the author or principle of *our natural life,* he being the Root of all mankind.

propagationem; ſic iſte princeps ſecundum ſpiritualem regenerationem; ille princeps ſecundum eſſe naturæ, iſte ſecundum eſſe gratiæ, &c. Eſt. in 1 Cor. 15. 45. Per.Mar. In 1 Cor. 15. 21. *Sunt tanquam duo principia, vel duæ radices generis humanæ.* Calv. apud Marl. in 1 Cor 15. 45.

Rom. 5. 19.

Videtur autem hoc loco duos homines Apoſtolus ab oculos ponere; ſpiritualem & animalem, quorum unus ab Adamo, alter vero a Chriſto derivatur; etenim quiſque noſtrum ut naturaliter vivit, ex radice Adam propagatur; qui vero ſpiritualiter, Chriſto inſitus eſt. Calvin. apud Marl. in 1 Cor.15.45.

The *Second* is the Author of our *Spiritual life,* he being the root of the *Elect,* the *head* and *Saviour* of his body the *Church.* Now as all men derive their *nature* from the *firſt Adam;* ſo alſo the Corruption that it hath contracted, being all covered over with it, conceived in ſinne, and borne in iniquity, filled with deprav'd affections and evil concupiſcence, breaking forth into ſinful

Eph. 5. 23.

Rom. 5. 12.

1 Cor. 15. 22.

Pſa. 51. 5.

Ephes. 2. 1, 2, 3.

finfull thoughts, words and actions; altogether defiled and unclean, and this *Corruption* derived from the firſt *Adam*, wherewith mans *nature* is tainted, is called the *old man* which muſt be put off with his deeds. The new *Man* growes out of the *ſecond Adam*, the effect of his Merit, *Grace* and *ſpirit*; compleat in all the parts of *righeouſneſſe*, and true *holineſſe*, filled with all heavenly Gifts in believing; this *new man* muſt be put on.

James 1. 14. 15

Col. 3. 9.

Rom. 15. 13.
Col. 3. 10.

Here the Apoſtle inſtructs us in the two fundamentals of *Chriſtianity*, *Mortification* and *Renovation*; and that his Exhortation may take the better, and make the deeper impreſſion, he uſes the *Metaphor* of *putting on and off*, that it may be knowne whoſe we are, and to whom we belong, whoſe *livery* we wear, and whoſe *Colours* we bear; if we be *Chriſts*, and belong to the ſecond *Adam* we muſt put on the *Garbe of Chriſtianity*, put

or.

on as the Elect of God, holy and beloved, Bowels of Mercies, kindnesse, humble-nesse of mind, meeknes, Long-suffer-ing.

Now of the *Graces, vertues, fruits* of the Spirit here mentioned, I have singled out *one,* a choise *one,* and it is *Meeknes,* of which I am now purposed to *speak,* and to *speak* of it as it is here propounded as a *Garment* to be *put on.*

Rom. 13.
14.
Gal. 3. 17.
Eph. 4 24.
Eph. 6 11.
And indeed Meeknesse is a *Garment* meet for a Christians wear; the *Apo-stle* hath suited it for us, and here commends it to us, to be *put on;* Put *on meekenesse.* It is a Metaphor where-with the Apostle seemes to be much delighted, by which he would give us to understand, that *vertues and vices* are *habits;* and *Habits* to the *minde* are as *Apparell* to the *body,* to be *put on and off.* And as a sordid ragged and filthy *Garment* doth vilifie, disgrace and dishonour the *body,* so do *vice* the *soule;* and as a clean and comely

ἐπιτέον οὖν
ὅτι πᾶσα ἀ-
ρετή ὅ ἂν
ᾗ ἀρετή,
αὐτό τε
εὖ ἔχον ἀ-
ποτελεῖ τὸ
ἔργον αὐτῶ
ἀποδίδωσιν
Arist. lib. 2.
Ethic. c. 6.
ἡ τοῦ ἀνθρώ-
πᾶ ἀρετή
ἕξιν ἂν ἕξις.
idem ibid.

Garmen

Garment doth honour and beautifie the *body*, fo do *vertues* beautifie and adorne the *foul*. And as it is unfightly and unfeemely to appear in publike on an high and folemne *day* in a torne and filthy *Garment*; fo in the light of the *Gofpel* and in the day of *Salvation* it is difhoneft and uncomely to be cloathed with *fin* and *vice*. *St Paul* condemnes it as a practice unreafonable and abfurd, that we who are dead to fin, fhould live any longer therein. The father could tell his fon now come to perfect years; *jamque hæc ætas aliam vitam, alios mores poftulat*; before the light of the *Gofpel*, the times of that ignorance God winked at: now the time of the *Gofpel* requires another courfe of *life*; let it fuffice to have mifpent the time paft; for the time to come, bring forth fruits worthy of amendment of life, faith *John* the Baptift. Sin no more (faith Chrift). *Iniquity* is a *difpa-*

Rom. 13 12

Rom. 6. 2

Teren. in Andr.

Acts 17. 30.

1 Pet. 4, 3. Mat. 3. 8. Luke 3. 8. Joh. 5. 14.

B 3 *ragement*

ragement to *Christianity*, and therefore let every one that calleth upon the name of the Lord depart from Iniquity; let not him that is filthy be filthy still, but let him cleanse himselfe from all filthinesse of the flesh and spirit, perfecting holinesse in the feare of God.

We must *strippe* our selves of the *Ragges* of *Old Adam,* (our sins and vices)by true and unfained repentance, and *put on* the *New Man,* which according unto God is Created in righteousnesse and true holinesse; *Justification* and *Sanctification,* which are *put on* by faith and love, wherewith the *Spouse* of *Christ* is all glorious within, is the ground work: her cloathing of *Wrought Gold* with raiment of needlework,wrought about with divers colours,are those severall *vertues and graces*,wherewith a *Christians conversation* is adorned, wherewith *the spouse of Christ* is decked,set forth

1 Tim. 2. 19.

Rev. 22. 11

2 Cor. 7. 1

Col. 3. 10.

Psal. 45. 13, 14.

forth in the *Canticles* in the *Rose* and Cant. 2.1. *Lillie*, the *Beril* and the *Saphire*,*rowes* of *Jewels*,*chaines* of *Gold*, *Borders* of Cant.1.10, 11. *Gold*, with *studs* of *Silver*, that is, Bowels of Mercies, kindnesse, humblenesse of mind, Meeknesse, long suffering, which the Colossians are, and we in them, here exhorted to put on.

Put on——*Meeknesse*.

Meekenesse, is the subject I am to speake to.

The use we are to make of it; It must *be put on*.

First of the subject, *Meeknesse*.

Meeknesse is of excellent use in our *Christian Conversation*; we can better be without our *Apparel* then with out it; for we can neither live Contentedly, nor die Comfortably

with-

Of Meeknesse,

with out Meekneffe. The holy Scripture highly commends it : Chrift
Crowns it with eternal bleffedneffe:
and God he will guide the meek in
judgement: and the meeke he will
teach his way: he will fave all the
Meeke of the earth, he will beautifie
the meeke with Salvation, and therefore *put on Meekneffe.*

And now, about to fpeake of
Meekneffe, I cannot begin better than
to crave a tafte of it in your *Atten-
tion,* in the words of the Apoftle,
Receive with *Meekneffe* the ingrafted
word, &c. In fpeaking of *Meekneffe,*
I will fay fomewhat of the *nature*
of it, and fomewhat of the *kinds* of
it.

For the *nature* of it, it is a *moral
vertue;* and *vertue,* to fpeak plainly,
is the right ufe of *Reafon* in the go-
verment of the *affections* and *paffions*
of the *foule;* for *knowledge* or *reafon*
being an *Act* of the *foule* refulting
from

Matth. 5.5.

Pfal. 25.9,

Pfal. 76. 9.

Pf. 149. 4.

Jam. 1. 21.

A ift. lib. 4.
Ethic. c. 5.

from the prime faculty the *mind* or
understanding, by difcourfe, doth
worke upon the Inferiour part of the
foule, the *will* and *affections*, informes
them in the *choice*, and rectifies them
in the *ufe* of things good and lawfull; hence comes *paſſion* to be ruled
by *reafon*, and *Reafon* to be guided by
Religion, and then is a **Chriſtian Man**
in his right temper when the Will
and Affections with all external actions are ordered according to the en-
lightened rule of *Rectified Reafon*.

Nil ſunt virtutes niſi ordinatæ affectiones. Bern.

Affections we cannot be without,
for they are *natural*, implanted in the
foule by the Maker of it, and the *ope-*
rations of them are not in vaine; for
of great ufe they are in *Religion*; they
are helps to *devotion* and to *dutie*; they are
the *wings of the foul* that carrie it up
to *Heaven* in *Devotion*; and they are

Affectiones utiles & à natura ad virtutem datæ. Juſt.
Lipſ. *in* Manuduc. *ad* Stoic. *Philo. lib.* 3 *diſſ. rt.* 7. 121. *b*.

Affectus velut ubertas eſt naturalis, ad quam cum verus cultus acceſſerit, ſtatim cedentibus vitiis, fruges virtutis oriuntur. Lact. l. 6, cap. 15. *ad* Juſt. Lipſ. *in* lib. 3. *Manud. ad* Sto. Philoſ. lib. 7.

the

Sine iis (i affectioni-bus) langue-bit omnis actio, & vis ac vigor animi resolvetur. Sen. lib. 1. de Ira. *Consule Ju-stum Lipsi-um in lib. 3. Manud. ad Stoicam Philosophi-am, dissert. 7. p. 121. b. Non enim ratio Om-nem pror-sus evelle-re pertur-bationem animi co-natur, cum*

the *Wind of the soul* that carries it on in dutie to God; were there not *affections,* we should neither *feare God,* nor *love Goodnesse,* nor *hate evil,* nor *desire hap-pinesse,* nor rejoyce *in the Lord,* nor be *zealous for* his glory; yet the *affec-tions* when they are in their Elevati-on, and grow into excesse, they de-generate into *passions* ; and *passions* are *fell* and *fierce*; *qua data porta ru-unt* ; upon any occasion break forth into distemper to the great disquiet and disturbance of the mind; Now *vertue* it is that does *Moderate,* finds out a meane, sets the *affections* in a right frame and temper ; brings into the *soul* a sweet *consent,* a heavenly *harmony,* a blessed *tranquillity.*

neque fieri id possit neque expediat: sed proponit finem ei quend m qui imponit ordinem, ingeneratque virtutes morales qua non sunt vacuitates motuum seu affectuum animi, sed eorum mediocritates, & concinnitates, &c. Plutarch. de virtute Moral. cap.10.

The *affections* and *passions* are of them-

themſelves unruly, head-ſtrong and violent; the *Wiſdome* and *Grace* which God gives to keep in and under theſe brutiſh *affections*, and ſweetly to temper them, is *vertue*; it bounds the *affections*, and binds up the *paſſions*, which like nocent *beaſts* (if they enjoy'd their own liberty) would do much harme and ſtrangely diſtemper the *world* as well as *man*.

Vide Plutarch. *Moral. in lib. de virtute morali. cap.* 13. *Bruta pars devincitur rationi, ac contemperatur, mirabili exornata obedientia, ac tranquillitate &c. Ita vehementes, furioſos rabidoſque motus ratio extinxit, &c. Per tot. cap. 20. lib. Plutarch. de virtute moral.*

The act of *vertue* then is to obſerve a golden mean between two extremes; and ſo we ſee in *temperance*, whereof *Meekneſſe* is a *ſpecies*, it is *liberal* without *laviſhneſſe*: *Frugal* without *Covetouſneſſe*: *Civil* without *ſullenneſſ*: *Stai'd* without *ſlothfulneſſe*: *affable* without *wantonneſſe*: *Modeſt* without *affectation*: *Shamefac'd* without *ignorance*: *Zealous* without

Τὴν δὲ ἀρετὴν τὸ μέσον χὴ ἐν ἑ σκεῖν, χὴ αἱρεῖδαι· *Ariſt. lib.* 3 *Ethic. c.* 6.

out Rashnesse : devout, and yet not *su-perstitious : precise,* but not *scrupulous : severe* but not *injurios: Austere,* but not *malicious : strict,* but not *Contentious;* in a word, it bridles *Anger,* mitigateth *griefe,* moderateth *joy,* that a man is neither over-joyd at the fruition, nor over-griev'd at the want or losse of things most dear and delightfull. It sheweth, *when,* and *how farre,* and *for what,* we may be *angry,* or *glad,* or *for-rowfull;* where we must *love,* and what we must hate; and seasons all our *Actions* with that due *time* which is appointed for every thing under the *sun.* And as for Meekenesse, it is chiefely shewn in *bearing and for-bearing.*

For he is Meeke that being provoked by *injuries,* doth patiently *beare,* and having opportunities of *Revenge* put into his hands, doth quietly *forbeare.*

The Meeke (saith Beza) are the gentle,

gentle, mild, and courteous, oppof'd to fuch as are wild, fierce and favage.

He is Meeke (faith *Hemingius*) that bridles his *affections*, who is not eafily provokt, and very ready to forgive an *injurie*.

He is Meeke (faith *Melanchthon*) that poffeffes his foul in *patience*, contents himfelf, and leaves *vengeance* unto *God*.

He is Meeke (faith *Calvin*) that refifteth not *evill*, but overcometh *evill* with *good*.

He is Meeke (faith *Ambro. Cath.*) who bridleth his *affections* that he is not *Angry*; or being *Angry*, finneth not.

He is Meeke (faith *Caffiodorus*) that fuffers all *wronges*, and *wrongs* none.

He is Meeke (faith *Hierom*) who is fo farre from doing hurt, that he thinks none.

By thefe defcriptions which thefe
Authors

Miles fuit qui cedunt improbrationibus, et non refiftunt in malo, fed vincunt in bono malum.
Aug. in Ser. Domini in monte.

Author give of the *Meeke*, we easily understand what the nature of *Meeknesse* is. It is a rare *vertue*, the true *Character* of a Saint, the proper *Garbe* of Election, Sanctification, Adoption.

By it we resemble God the *Father* who is the *Father* of *Mercies*, and God of all Consolation.

2 Cor.1.3.

By it we resemble God the *Son*, whose proper Attribute is to be *Meeke* and *lowely*.

Mat.11.29

By it we resemble *God the Holy Ghost* the *Comforter*, who to shew the meek and Gentle properties of his nature, appeared in the shape of a *dove*.

Mat.3.16.

It is a Certaine signe of *heavenly-mindednesse*; for as the superior part of the world, and that which is nearest the *starres*, hath neither Clouds nor *Stormes*, nor any *Meteors* engendered

Pars superior mundi & ordinatior, ac propinqua sideribus, nec in nubem cogitur, nec in tempestatem impellitur, nec versatur in turbinem: omni tumultu caret, inferiora fulminant. Seneca lib.3. de Ira.cap.6.

in

in it, nor is it subject to perturbation; *omni tumultu caret;*all is calm & quiet there:whereas thundering,lightning, stormes,and tempests,are engendered in the lower parts. So the good Christian whose Conversation is in heaven, whose thoughts are above the *Clouds,* and is mov'd with nothing here below is free from Mallice, envie, revenge, hatred, disdain, and is alwayes *Calme, quiet, modest, mild,gentle.*

Meekenesse it is placed betweene two *extreames.*

On the one side is *Anger,* a hot fierce and fiery *passion.*

On the other side *Lenitude,* or rather dulnesse and stupidity, a slow, idle, dull affection.

The former of these I may compare to *fire;* the Prophet hath done

ἔςι ἡ ἐπι-
εἰ ὀργὴ
ὑπερβολὴ
ἡ ἔλλεψις
ἡ μισότης·
μηδὲν δὲ
ἀναρώνυμων
ὄντων τὸν
μέσον πρᾶ-
ολέγοντες,
τὴν μισό-
τητα πραι-
ότητα κα-

λέσωμεν· τῶν δὲ ἄκρων ὁ μὲν ὑπερβάλλων ὀργίλ Θ ἔςω. ἡ δὲ κα-
κία ὀργιλότης, ὁ ἢ ἐλλεί πως ἀόργητος τίς· ἡ δ' ἔλλεψις ἀοργα-
σία. Arist. lib. 2. Ethic. cap. 7

it

it for me : *shall thy wrath burn like fire?* the latter unto *water*, which of it selfe without an *higher Principle* of Nature, is cold and chill, very hardly either moved to *good*, or remov'd from *evil*; thus the Meek man is set in the midst of evil : if he incline to one hand, he is in danger to be scorch'd with the burning fire of *anger :* if to the other hand, to be drown'd in the dead sea of dulnesse or senselesse *stupidity*; *medio tutissimus*; no safety but in a *meane* between the two, and that is Meeknefs.

Thus the *meek man* must passe through fire and water ; so the Psalmist speaking of the injuries Gods people endured, sets forth how hardly they were put to it, We went (saith he) through fire, and through water: but *thou broughtest us out into a wealthy place.* The *meek man* in the midst of mischief hath the promise of of Gods prefence and protection, *Ifa. 43. 2. When thou paffeft through the water, I will be with thee : and through the rivers, they fhall not overflow thee : when thou walkeft through the fire, thou fhalt not be burnt, neither fhall the flame kindle upon thee ;* and this for the *Nature of Meekneffe.*

Ifa. 43. 2.

For *the kinds of* Meekneffe; There is a *Meekneß* towards *God* , and a *Meekneffe* towards *man.*

For *Meekneffe* refpecteth both *God* and *man* ; it fets the foul in a right temper to *God* , and alfo to *man.*

Meekneffe towards *God,* is a willing and ready fubmiffion of our *judgements* and *affections* to the will and pleafure of *God* in all things, without fretting, murmuring or repining.

For as we muft not queftion the the *Fuftice of God* in fuffering the wicked to *profper:*

So neither muft we *murmure* at

C   the

the godnesse and providence of God in suffering the *godly to be afflicted.* Why God doth suffer it to go *ill* with the *good*, and *well* with the *bad*; that the worst *prosper* best, and the best *suffer* most, is a secret of divine *provid'nce* which we must submit unto, not question: knowing that *wicked* men, the more happy they are, the more *wretched* they are; for what greater *Wretchedness* can there be then to prosper in evil *Courses* ? Gods dealings in this particular, & his dispensation of outward blessings is both *wise* and *just*. Why God doth so or so, he is not bound to give us an acconnt; *secret* he may be, unjust he cannot be.

Here then let us acquiesce; the Justice of *God* herein is not to be accused of partiality, as if he lightly passed by, and *slightly* passed over the sins of some, as an *Accepter of persons* (when God knows there is nothing in their persons he should accept) but we must
                                              let

et *God* alone with his own *Work,* and
iffer him to take his own *way;* for
hough he permit the wicked to *prof-*
er, to proceed and go on in an un-
iterrupted state of outward *felicity*
id immunity from *dangers;* though
e seeme to order and dispose all oc-
hsions and occurents for their *ad-*
ancement in this present world; and
though theybe not unfurnished of
:etences both plausible and pleasing
is a thing *Customable* and *Common*
the world, and therefore the
sse questionable, and more excu-
ble in the *judgments* of *corrupt*
en) entertaining any means, un-
rtaking any condition, laying hold
any advantage, sticking at no-
ing that may help or further their
terest, or mount them to the top
their *desires;* yet that *light,* and
ose *notions* they labour to *quench,*
d *eradicate,* breaks in upon them;
d many times iu the midst of their

C 2 con-

confidence they are brought into
ftraights ; and at length thofe *dread-
ful curfes* and maledictions , which
continually *dogge them,* will furely o-
vertake them, either at their *paffage*
out of this life, or *entrance* into another,(though *Babylon* fit as a Queen,
and fee no forrow, yet God doth
know her day is coming) So God
may *connive* at them, he *confents* no
to them : He may feeme to pav
their way to *hell* with oyle and but
ter: fuffer them to play with th
Waffe and *Hornets* neft, till they b
ftung to death ; they have all thing
they can defire, but as *nets* and *fnare*
and a *curfe* withal, as the *Ifraelit*
had *Quailes;* we fee their open *prid*
we fee not their fecret *pinches.* Er
vie not therefore the profperity
wicked men , *fret not thy felfe b
caufe of evil doers,* but obferve tl
Pfal. 37. 1 end of the Lord.

Surely their *condition* is unce

ain, they have no fure ftanding; God
ath fet them in flippery places, and
heir foot fhall flip in due time, which *Pfal.73.*
iould invite them to *repentance*, or a *18.*
reater *fall*: and therefore that God *Pfal.34.*
oth fuffer them, and fufpend his *35.*
engeance, as it doth commend his
atience and abundant *clemencie*; fo
iould it filence our *murmuring*,
aufe us applaud his *wifdom* and
ftice, to be contented with his dea- *Job. 21.7.*
igs, and put on *meeknefs*. *Pfal.10.*
  I know how many good men have *13.* *Pfal.73.3.*
een ftrangely affected at Gods do- *&c.*
gs in this kind. *Job* and *David*, *Jer. 12.1.*
d *Afaph* and *Jeremiah* with others.
it after a thorough fearch and exa-
ination of Gods waies, they refted
erewith not *contented* only but
inkful, acknowledging their er-
rs and overfight, and admiring the
tice of heaven, who fooner or la- *Gen.15.*
 will not fuffer the wicked to go *16.*
punifhed, When their iniquitie
         C 3   is

Rev. 14.
15.
is full, and the harvest of their fins
ripe, God will put in his ficle, and
they fhall foon be cut down as the
Pfal. 37.2
grafs, and wither as the green herb.
And if they fcape free in this life as
feldome they do, yet in the life to
come they fhall meet with *wrath* and
vengeance in full *vials*: and therefore though *flout and ftubborn finner,*
do think to bear up themfelves a-
gainft the *juftice of heaven*, yet know
there is placed over them an *armed*
revenger who will not acquit the
wicked of his doings; for Gods *pati-*
ence and filence have fixed bounds
he will plead his own caufe, will righ
his Saints, and punifh the wicked after their defervings: For the tim
when he will do it, that we muf
leave to *God*; it is not for us to kno
the *times* and *feafons*, which the Fa
Acts 1.7.
ther hath kept in his own powe
All that we know is, that there
truth in Gods *word*, and *power* in h
han

and. He is not (as *Cæcilius* in *Minutius Felix* alledges) *invalidus ut iniquus*, unable and cannot, or unjuſt and will not ; but he both can and will make good his word upon them. For the time when, and the means how he will do it, we muſt leave to his ordering : we have ſeen Meteors blaze by night, and periſh the next morning with the *Riſing Sun*. They have their *Heaven here*, till ſuddenly the *Oracles* of God take place, and then in a *moment* they tumble into the *pit*.

Their *good* is not in their *hand*, for a *moment* ſhall devour them with their *portions*. Though they ſcape for a time, thinking, ſpeaking, doing what they pleaſe, wallowing as *Swine* in the mire, and fatted as *Buls of Ba-n* for the day of ſlaughter; yet when the *Heavens* ſhall melt, and the Mountains be moved, what covert ſhall hide them from that *wrath*

Pſal. 55.
23.
Job. 21.
15.
Pſal. 37.
9, 10.
Pſal. 73.
19
2 Pet. 3.
22.
Pſal. 22.
12.
2 Pet. 2.
12.
Luk. 23.
30.
Rev. 6.16.
Iſa. 2.19.
Hoſ. 10.8.

C 4   which

*Victima
sacra Deo
comburi-
tur, abripit
offam Hinc
Aquila, ad
pullos fert
que ineun-
da suos; Fa-
tali igniculus prædæ
imperceptus
adhæsit,
Sacrilega-
qis e sacer.
devorat ignis
opes.
Hab. 2. 6.*

*Psal. 37.
14.
Psal. 31.
24.
Ila. 28. 16.
Raro ante-
cedentem
scelestum
deseruit
pede pœna
c'auda.
Ro. 12. 19.*

which they shall not be able to *abide
or evade?*

No mans misery then being greater then theirs whose impiety is most fortunate, there is greater cause for them to bewail their own unhappinefs, then others to *envy or murmure* at their happy estate.

There is a *woe* for him that encreaseth that which is not his; we read of the *Eagle* snatching a morsel from the *Altar*, carried therewith the *Coal* that consum'd her *nest*, and burnt up her *young ones:* means ill gotten will one day more *torment* a man, than ever it did *enrich* him; and a succeding age (if not before) shall see them melt to *nothing.*

In the mean time let us take the Psalmists advice, to tarry the Lords leasure, and to wait his good pleasure; *For they that believe, will not make hast. Vengeance is Gods, he will repay;* if *wickednefs* go before, *vengeance*

eance is not far behind : it follows :lofe at the heels of wickednefs ; *hough hand go in hand, yet fhall not the vicked go unpunifhed.* *For God will vound the head of his enemies, and the hairy fcalp of fuch an one as goeth on ?ill in his wickednefs.*

I know fome are too *hafty,* and would prevent God ; will take upon them to prefcribe him *waies* and *means,* like the two fons of *Zebedie,* fire they muft have from heaven : our Saviour reproves their *rafh and heady Zeal,* and tels them they know not of what *fpirit* they are. *Chrift* was their *Mafter* ; and it is fit the *Difciples* fhould be of their *Mafters fpirit.* It was a prime leffon he would have them learn, *Learn of me for I am meek and lowly* : it feems St. *Paul* had well cond this leffon, and therefore commends it to the pra- ctife of his *Brethren* as the beft *ornament* of their profeffion.

The

Pro. 11. 21.

Pfal. 68. 21.

Luk. 9. 54.

Luk. 9. 55.

Mat. 11. 29.

Gal. 6. 1.

The ſpirit of *Chriſt* is a ſpirit of *meekneſs; He came not to deſtroy mens* Lu.9.56. *lives,but to ſave them.* And ſuch a ſpirit beſt becomes them who call themſelves by the name of *Chriſt;* they are much to ſeek who think *Chriſt* will have his *cauſe* vindicated with fire and ſword. That the enemies of *Chriſt* deſerve no better, no man doubts; but if every one ſhould have his deſert, the world would have an end;and therefore *Peter* muſt Mat.26. up with his *ſword: James* and *John* 52. muſt out with their fire: there will be uſe of both, but they muſt ſtay his leaſure until he call who hath the command of both.

But *men* are impatient, think the time long, which meaſured by their diſtempered appetites, they flie out into *paſsion*, and accuſe God of *ſlackneſs*, and think they are wrong'd, if they be not preſently reveng'd,when their betters forbear and are ſtill unreveng'd:

reveng'd : we dayly fee it; *God is pro-* Pfal.7.11.
voked every day, he fuffers *much,* and
he fuffers *long, as a Cart is preffed that* Amos 2.
is full of fheaves; He bears the *fins* 13.
of men, and forbears his *Judgments,*
not this *day,* and the next, but how Mat.23.
often? he bore with the *Ifraelites* 37.
fourty years ; with the old *world* one Pfal.95.
hundred and twenty *years*; and ftill 10.
every *day,* and all the *day* long, he Gen.6 3.
reacheth forth the *hand of mercy* to a Ifa 65.2.
gain-faying *people.* God hath *ven-* Ro.10 21.
geance in his *power,*but not in his *will*;
if he were as impatient as man is, the
Idolater in his *Sacrifice* : the *fwearer* in
his *blafphemy* : the *unclean perfon* in
his *Adultery* : the *formalift* in his
Hypocrify : the *Epicure* in the midft
of his *drunkennefs* and *gluttony* : and
Tyrants in their *rage and cruelty* had
been confum'd.

God is *wronged,* yet he *endures* it :
God fuffers, what no man would *en-*
dure. Nay,the *Son of God, Jefus Chrift*
our.

nor Lord is not yet avenged of the *injuries* that have been done unto him, the *Indignities* that have been caft upon him: the *Blafphemies* fpoken againft his name; the *Crueltie's* done againft his fervants ; How long Lord holy and true? oh! the *meeknefs, gentlenefs and patience* of a bleffed Saviour, to fuffer a company of *worms* and *vermine* upon earth to *blaſpheme* that name, whom all the hoft of heaven do adore: *He is judged of men: but he judgeth no man:* and although the *Father* hath committed all *judgmente* to the *Son*; yet the *Son* fufpendeth his *judgment* until the appointed time, to which he hath referved the unjuft to be punifhed, when he fhall be revealed from *heaven* with his *mighty Angels*, in flaming fire, taking vengeance on all them that know not *God,* and obey not the Gofpel of our *Lord Jefus Chriſt.* And the *holy Ghoſt* is *greived*

Rve.6.10.
Jo.8.15.
Joh. 5.22.
Act.17.31.
2 Pet.2.9.
2 Thef. 1. 7, 8, 9.

ved every day, *refifted, defpited, blaf-* phemed; his motions *quenched*: his infpirations *fmothered*: his operations *interrupted*: yet ftill he waits, expects, ftands at the dore, and knocks: thus he doth yet, but thus he will not al-waies do; *the fpirit of the Lord* will not alwaies ftrive with *man*: for that he is but *flefh*: he will *withdraw*, and will at laft give place to that heavy *indignation*, which fhall break forth from the *prefence of the Lord*, and *from the glory of his power.* Let us do as God does, judg not before the time; he is *righteous* in all his waies, and the difpenfations of his providence are moft *wife and good.* Wherefore let us not judg amifs in *repining or mur-muring*, either at our own *fufferings*, or at his *long-fuffering* thofe that are not his. But let every one in the fear of God, be careful to work out their own Salvation: and as for *Gods enemies* and theirs, let them pray for
their

Eph 4.1.3.
Act.7. 50.
Heb.10.29
Mat.12.
31.
Lu.12.10.
Act. 18 6.
1 Thef. 5.
19.
Rev.3.20.
Gen. 6. 3.

2 Thef. 1.
9.
1 Cor.4.
5.
Pfal. 145.
17.

Phil.2.12.

their *conversion*, and not solicite their *subversion* before the *appointed time.*

Peter was chek'd for his *curiosity* in demanding concerning *John*, what shall *this man* do? If I will (*faith Christ*) that he stay till I come, what is that to thee? follow thou me. What and if it be the will of God both tares and wheat should grow up together to the harvest ? What and if God willing to shew his wrath, and to make his power known, endure with much patience the vessels of wrath fitted to destruction ? shall man repine at the *doings* of his *Maker ?* rather in all *humility* let us submit our selves to his most just and wise *designments*, rest contented with his proceedings, and *put on meekness.*

Secondly, as we must not call in Question the *justice* of God in suffering the *wicked* to prosper, so neither must we murmure at the *goodness* and *providence* of God in suffering
the

Joh. 21. 21.

Mat. 13. 30.

Ro. 9. 22.

the *godly* to be afflicted.

For *affliction* is the Saints lot ; the portion of the *Righteous* ; the *Legacy* Chrift bequeathed his own Difciples: in the world ye fhall have trouble ; and in the whole *book* of God we read of *one* that finned not , but not of any *one* that fuffered not.

Jo.16.20;
33.
Jo.15.20.
Pf.34.19.
Act.14.22
1 The.3.3.
2 Tim.3.
12.
2 Cor.5.
21.
Job. 14.1.
Eccl.40.1.
1Pe. 4.12.

Nullus fervus Chrifti, fine tribula ione eft; fi putas te non habere perfecutiones. nondum cœpifti effe Chriftianus, Aug.

Si exceptus es paffion flagellorum, exceptus es a munere.e fi ir um. Idem de paff. V.de Hieron. *ad Euftoch.*

And therefore *reafon* fhould teach us to *put on meeknefs,*to fuffer *affliction* with a quiet and contented *mind:* for who can think to efcape that which hath befaln *all ?* and not to *do willingly,* what muft of *necefsity be done?*

Fer quod fors præfens tibi fert;n m, ferre recufans te lædes : & te fors tam n abripiet Bafilius. *Proximus Deo plenus eft flagellis.*Amb. *Clem. Alex. lib. 2. Stromat.*

And *Religion* teaches that it is the way of all *Saints*; no man ever came
to

to *heaven* but by it : and if we be no
worſe us'd then *Gods beſt beloved
friends,* we have no cauſe of *complaint.*

See *firſt* what they *endur'd* : and
how they *endur'd* it.

They endured *ſorrows* not to be
endur'd : they had tryal of *cruel
mockings* and *ſcourgings* : yea moreover of Bonds and impriſonments :
they were *ſtoned* : they were *ſawn* a-
Heb.11.
36,37,38. ſunder : were tempted : were *ſlain*
with the *ſword* : they wandered about
in *ſheep-skins,* and *goat-skins* ; being
deſtitute, afflicted, tormented. This
they *ſuffered.*

How *ſuffered* they this ? They
went away *rejoycing* that they were
Act.5.41. accounted worthy to *ſuffer* for the
name of *Chriſt.* And the *Apoſtle* tels
Heb.10.34 us of the *Hebrews,* that they *ſuffered*
with joy the ſpoiling of their *goods.*
And if we look higher, and take our
direction from a *clearer ſight,* let us
look

look to *Jesus* the author and finisher of our faith : no mans *sufferings* were ever like his (while he lived upon *earth*;) though he walked *unblamably*, never hurt *any*, pitied *all*, helped *all* that came unto *him*, yet he was not *believed* in his *word*, he was *reproached* in his *life*, *hated* in his *person*, *greived* in his *spirit*, the whole way of the *world* went against *him*, yet his *meekness* was as great as his *sufferings*. To *suffer* what he *suffer'd* with *patience*, was much: but to *suffer* with *silence*, was much more : many times in the midst of their *afflictions*, men use to releive themselves with *complaints* : But *He was led as a lamb to the slaughter, and as a sheep is dumb before the shearer, so opened he not his mouth.* There was no *complaint* in his *lips* : no *clamour* in his *tongue* : he did not *cry*, neither was his *voice* heard in the *streets*; and Saint *Paul* would have all *Christian men* to be

D of

Heb.12. 2.
Lam.1.12.
Joh.8. 46.
Joh.10.32
Mat 9.36.
Mat.14.14
Mat.15.32
Mat.4. 23.
Joh.1.11.
Joh.5.44.,
46.
Joh 6. 64.
& 12.37.
Mat.11.19
Mar.3. 22.
Mat.17.17
Joh.11.33
Mar.3.5.
Psal.2.1.
Isa.53.7.

Isa.42 23.

Phil. 2. 5. of the same *temper:* for hereunto are we call'd (saith Saint *Peter*) to be partakers of his *sufferings* ; for he *suffered* for us, leaving us an *example* that we should follow his *steps.*

1 Pet. 2. 21. Not only to *suffer* what he did : but to *suffer* as he did, with the same *quietneß* of mind, *meekneß* and *humility.*

Can there be a stronger inducement to *meekneß* in the midst of *afflictions* then the example of *Chriſt?* The Author to the *Hebrews* adviseth to *conſider him that endur'd ſuch contra-* Heb.12.3. *diction of ſinners leſt, ye be wearied and faint in your minds.* Thus whether we look upon the example, (our *Saviour Chriſt*) or the virtue exemplified (*meekneß*) both are worthy our imitation. Such a *virtue* were to be imitated in any *perſon* : such a *perſon* to be followed in any *virtue.* So then the more *meek* a man is, the more like *Chriſt* he is, & consequently
ly

ly the more *heavenly* and *happy* he is ; and therefore *put on meekneſs.*

Our enemy the *Devil* knows how uſeful a *garment* our *meekneſs* is, and therefore would rob us of it.

God ſuffer'd him to practice upon *Job* ; but by all the loſſes and croſſes he brought upon him, he could not provoke him to *murmuring and im-patience.* He had thought to have given his *meekneſs* the foyl, by laying his *hand* upon his *body.* For he ſaid, *put forth thine hand upon his bone, and upon his fleſh, and he will curſe thee to thy face.*

But as cunning as the *tempter* was here, he was deceived : for *Job* was refolv'd nor to *curſe* God though he kild him : he knew the utmoſt extent of *Sathans* power was but his body, and if it muſt be ſo, he is willing to lay it down with *meekneſs,* in aſſurance to have it reſtor'd : and to receive it again, compleat in all the

D 2   parts

Job.1.12.

Job.1.22.

Job.2.5.

Job.2.10.

Job.13.15

Job.19.2 26, 27.

parts of it. Though *Job* could object his *innocency* against *Satans calumny*, he will not therefore presently *murmur* and call in question *Gods goodneß*, but will attend with *patience*, the further manifestation of his good will and pleasure; and in the mean time put his mouth in the dust. Oh then when *God* threatens, let us meet him on our *knees*, and like obedient *Children* kiss the *rod*, and give glory to the *hand* that guids it, and say with holy *Job*, *Shall we receive good from God: and shall we not receive evil also?* *God is* the fountain of all *goodneß*, and if he be pleased to turn our *sweetneß* into a little *bitterneß*, shall we repine at the omnipotent *wisdom* of our *Maker?* *God* is so *good*, that he would suffer none evil to befal us, except he were so *wise*, as to know how to extract *good* out of *evil*, and to make the *afflictions* of his *Children* (like so many ~~parallel~~ *lines*) meet in the

center

Ad aliquem usum sanctorum ordinatur omnis actus impiorum a summo Deo, a qui pro sui regiminis æquitate, bene utitur etiam malis, ut qui suo arbitrio injuste vivunt, illius judicio juste disponantur. Aug. contra Fauft. Manic. lib. 16.cap.21.

center of his *glory* and their *good* : making *all things work together for the*
good of them that are his.

There are divers *cases* men frame
to themselves, which causes them.
to entertain their *sufferings* with *im-*
patience.

First, they are not thorowly per-
swaded their *afflictions* are from *God,*
and therefore they fly out and are
unquiet, they blame their *stars* , they
rail on *fortune* , and after a brutish
manner like unreasonable *creatures*
they let fly at the *stone,* and never
eye the *hand* that sent it (Subordinate *means,* second causes, and such
men. and *things* which God only
makes *instrumental* to his *providence*)
they imputing their *sufferings* to any
thing rather than *God*; wheras indeed
they should look beyond all things
below unto an hand *above* that guideth
all: for what can any thing *do,* or *be,*
without him, who is the *first Agent*

Rom.8.28

Amos.4.6,
7,8,9.

Amos.3.6.

D 3ᵐ   and

Job.5.6. and original of all *being?* both pro-
ducing and imploying *subordinate*
means to his own *wise purposes :* con-
triving and fetching about all *things,*
and acting them according to own
will?

This not well confidered, but
men in their *afflictions* poring too
much upon immediate *Instruments,*
and fecond *caufes,* break out into
pafsion and *impatience,* fretting and
fuming and meditating *revenge :* but
when they confider they have to do
with *God,* this filences all *complaints,*
makes the *fufferer* quietly to fubmit,
Pfa.39.9. and to acknowledg the *hand* of *God,*
Ifai.4.55. and that there is no ftriving with his
Maker ; when Saint *Pauls* friends un-
derftood the mind of *God* concerning his *Bonds* and *Imprifonment,* and
that no fear of *danger* could divert
him from his peremptory refolution
of going to *Hierufalem ,* they ceafed
to importune him, fubmitting unto
the

the *will* of the *Lord*, the difpofer and orderer of all *events*. And *David* was filent when he was fatisfied concerning his *fufferings*, that they were from *God* ; he laies his hand upon his *mouth*, and faies no more, *But I became dumb and opened not my mouth, for it was thy doing.*

Yea, in our bleffed *Saviours fufferings* the gates of *hell*, and powers of *darkncfs*, the *Jews* and *Judas*, *Pilate* and *Caiphas* , the *Priefts* and the *Soldiers*, active *inftruments* all of them , but their *power* was derived from *God*, their *malice* limited by *God* ; and they *did* that, and no more could they *do*, but what the *hand of God* and his *Counfel* determined before to be *done* : and all that was *done* unto him, and all that was *fuffered* by him, he acknowledges to be *Gods doing*, not *theirs* , the forrow wherewith the Lord afflicted him. Could we take this courfe in

Act.21.13
14.

Pfal.39 9

See all the
Gofpels,
Mat.26.
27.
Mar.14. 15
Luk: 22.23
Joh. 18. 19
Joh 19.11

Joh. 19 36

Act.2. 23

Lam.1.12

D 4 our

Rev. 3. 19.
2 Pet. 2. 9.
Pfal. 119.
75.
Mat. 10.
29.
Luk. 12. 6.
7.
our private and publick *calamities*, to take them as from *God*, the effects of his *love*; *wisdom* and *faithfulneß*, without whose *providence* a *sparrow* fals not to the *ground*, nor a *hair* from our *heads*: that these things are *done* unto us in singular *wisdom*, and special *love* to our *souls*: so *David* took them; I know (saith he) *O Lord, that thy Iudgments are right: and that thou in faithfulneß haſt af-*

Pſ. 119. 75.
flicted me. This will quiet our hearts, and suſtain onr *spirits* in the midſt of *afflictions*: *Be ſtill and know*

Pſa. 46. 10
that I am God. When *Mauritius* the Emperor, his wife and five ſons were taken, his *wife* and *five ſons* put to *death* before his *eyes*, and *himſelf*

Pſa'm 119
137.
Secreta ſſe
poſſunt ju-
dilia Dei,
injuſta ſſe
non poſſunt.
Aug.
waiting for the like fatal *blow*, concluded thus, *Righteous art thou O Lord, and right are thy Iudgments.* let our thoughts quietly reſt here: the cauſe of *Gods Iudgments* may be *ſecret,* and unknown to us, they

can-

not be *unjuft*; how *unjuft* foe-
ver the *Agents* be, by which the *juft*
God fcourges his own, who *defpight-*
fully do their own *wils*, whilft they
unwittingly do Gods.

Confider not how *unjuft* the A-
gent is that *gives* the *blow*, as how
juft God is that *guides* it.

And this would be our *meditation*
in al *cafes* to think whofe *hand ftrikes*:
whether in *Epidemical* vifitations,
of famine, peftilence, or the fword;
or *perfonal*, as ficknefs, poverty,
forrow, lofs or crofs; and to con-
clude the *blow* is *Gods*, whofoever
or whatfoever is us'd as the *weapon.*
Yea, it comes not without *defert*, becaufe *God* is *juft*: nor fhall be without profit, becaufe *God is good.*

It is to be confidered likewife that
God who fendeth *afflictions*, ordereth
them to very *good ends*, as namely, to
conform *men* to the *Image of Chrift**,
who was a man of forrows and learn'd

Confule de hac re Philip. Melan. locis communibus Theologicis decalamitatibus & de cruce, ubi tractat de quatuor generibus afflictionum;

Τιμωρίαι, δοκιμασίαι, μαρτύριον, λύτρον *Non venit fine merito quia Deus eft juftus; nec erit fine commodo, quia Deus eft bonus. Aug.*

ἵνα μάθωμεν μὴ εἰς ἄνθρωπον βλέπειν ἀλλ᾽ εἰς Θεὸν ἀποβλέπειν.

Bafil. *Homil.* 21.* Heb. 2. 10 Luk. 24. 26. Ifa. 53. 3. Heb. 5. 8

Ex-

Donis suis Deus flagella permiscet, ut nobis omne quod nos in seculo delectabit, amarescat: &c. Greg. super Ezec. vide Sanctum Hieronymum Tom. 9. ep. 20. Anne est aliquid tam durum,&c. ut misericordiam exigamus? Aug.in Psa. 39. ad gratiam commendandam. Aug.de verbis Domini. Omnis divina percussio purgatio in nobis vitæ præsentis est. Greg. moral. lib.18. cap. 13.

Adversitas probatio virtutis est, non indicium reprobationis. Greg. in Regist.

1 Pet. 1.7. Rom. 5,3 4.

Patientia in prosperis nullus est usus Greg. moral. lib. 11. cap. 19. in malis quæ quisque patitur, non in bonis quibus fruitur, opus est patientia. Aug. in Joh. 12.4. vide Tert. de pœnit. cap. 10. ad explorandum, deplorandum, implorandum. Alsted. System. Theol. Aug.in Ps. 49. idem lib. 2. confess. opus enim est ad sui notitiam experimento,&c. Sen.lib.de Pro. Deus utique qui quem corripit diligit quando corripit ad hoc corripit ut emendet. Cyp. lib.4. ep. 4.

perience by the things he suffered; *To wean them from the love of this world:* to make them fit for *mercies:* to make his *mercies* more choice and dear unto them: to soften & melt their *hearts*; to purge out their *corruptions:* to kindle their *zeal:* to inflame their *devotion:* to strengthen their *faith:* to exercise their *hope:* to beget in them *charity and compassion* towards others: to make tryal of their *patience:* to break the *pride* of their *spirits,* that they may search and try their waies: to teach them to *deny* themselves, and cast off their *carnal confidence:* to

amend

mend whatſoever he finds amiſs: making them more wary of their *ſteps:* and to have their *converſation* in the world more *humble* and void of *offence*: with a greater hatred and deteſtation of *ſin*: and with a more fervent deſire and care to ſerve and pleaſe *God*: yea, *God* orders their *afflictions* for the exerciſe of the *graces* he hath beſtow'd upon them in this *life:* and for the further encreaſe of the *glory* he hath prepared for them in the *life to come.*

Deus corruptelam noſtram non patitur longius procedere, ſed plagis ac verberibus emendat. Lact. div. Inſt. lib. 3. c.17 Aug. in Pſ. 21. in Pſa 60. n ſc m. ad Liſpium. Salvian. de provid. Dei. Greg. lib. 11. moral. *Quos amat emendat, ſceleri ique impon t habenas.* Bapt. Man. de fortuna Gonzagæ *Cavendum eſt vulnus quod cum dolore curatur. Adverſa corporis, remedia ſunt animæ* Iſidorus de ſummo bono, lib. 3. *Ad virtutes ſpectat tribulations fortiter ſuſtinere.* Bern. ſuper Cant. ſerm. 85. *In Deo certa eſt fiducia, quando pro bono adverſitas additur, in hoc mundo recipitur, ut pulchrior merces in r tribution ne æterna ſervetur.* Greg. in Regiſtro. vide etiam Greg. mor. lib. 26. cap. 18.

Men therefore being once perſwaded of this, that all *afflictions* are from *God*, of his *ſending*, and of his *ordering*, they ſhould take up the reſolution of old *Ely*,   *It is the Lord,*

let

1 Sam.3. 18.

let him do what ſeemeth him good ; for whatſoever ſeemeth *good* to him, is *good* indeed, howſoever it ſeem to us.

Thus *God* chaſteneth us for our *profit,* (ſaith the Author to the *Hebrews*)& therfore we ſhould accept of his *corrections,* not with *meekneſs* only, but with *thankfulneſs.* So *David* thanks *God* for his *troubles* as for a ſpecial *favour*; *It is good for me that I have been in trouble :* and pronounces ſuch for *bleſſed, Bleſſed are they whom thou chaſteneſt :* For *Gods love* is the ground of all *bleſſedneſs*; and that may conſiſt with *affliction,* inſomuch that *God loveth* not whom he *afflicteth not :* So that *afflictions* are *tokens of Gods* love, *markes of Adoption, teſtimonies of eternal happineſs,* and therefore we ſhould prepare our ſelves patiently to endure them, *by putting on meekneſs.*

But there are ſome *caſes* eſpecially

Heb.12. 10.

Pſal. 119. 71.
Pſa.94.12

Heb.12.6.
Rev.3.19.
Pro.3.11, 12.
Heb. 12.7.
Job. 5. 17.
Jam.1.12.

ly

ty wherein *men* are apt to *murmure*; as *firft* when their *troubles* are *extream*, very *great*, and *many*, and hard to be *endur'd*.

Secondly, When they are *tedious* and of long *continuance*, when a man can fee no end of his *troubles*, find no *way* to get out of them.

Or Thirdly, when they are *alone*, *fuffering* what no man elfe, when no man befides themfelves doth *fuffer*.

Here are hard *cafes* put: yet fuch as the beft *Saints* of *God* have undergone.

This was *Davids caufe*; read the 38 and the 88 *Pfalm*, and fee into what a fad and forlorn *condition David* was brought: what heavy *complaints* and grieveous *lamentation* doth he make, that the *Arrows* of God did ftick faft in him, that his *hand* preffed him fore, that there was no *foundnefs* in his *flefh*, that he was bowed

Pfal.38.2.

3.

6.

11.

Pfal.88.3.

7.

bowed down greatly, and went mourning all the day long: that there was none to comfort him; lovers, friends, neighbours, acquaintance stood a far off, that his foul was full of troubles, that his life drew nigh unto the grave; that the wrath of God lay heavy upon him: that he afflicted him with all his waves.

This was *Jobs cafe*, for he acknowledgeth he wanteth *words* to expref's his *grief:* for (faith he) *the Arrows of the Almighty are within me, the poyfon whereof drinketh up my spirit; the terrors of God fet themselves in array againft me.* That Moneths of vanity and wearifome nights were appointed to him; That he could not reft day nor night; But was full of toffings too and fro; fo difquieted he was, that he curfed the day of his nativity, and wifhes that he had been as an untimely birth: or

Job.6.4.

Job 7.3.

4.

Job.3.4.5.
6.7.8.9.10

as

as infants vvhich never fee the light; Job. 3.16.
yea his diftemper grevv to that
heighth that he breaks forth and
cries out, O that it vvould pleafe God Job. 6.9.
O uinam
è noftro
fecedere
corpore
poffim.
to deftroy me, that he vvould let
loofe his hand and cut me off. Thus
Jobs fufferings vvere great, vvhich
vvere the caufe of much *difquiet* to
that *good-man* : his *life* vvas full of Job.14.1.
Job.1.---.
Job.2. 7.
Job.7.11.
14, 15
mifery, he *fuffered loffe* in his *Eftate*,
fear in his *children*, *pain* in his *body*,
horror in his *foul*, *difcouragement* from
his *friends.* Now to fettle the mind.& Job.16. 2.
quiet it in the midft of thefe *troubles*,
vvhen at any time they come thick
and threefold:

It muft be confidered that *God is*
with his *children* in their greateft
afflictions, and his prefence fweet- Ifa.42. 2.
3.
ens every *condition* ; for where he is,
he is not as an idle fpectator of their
miferies : but there is with him *help*, Ifa.50. 7.
and *comfort*, and *light*, and *life*.

Where he is, no *evil* can be *fear-*
ed,

Psal.23.4.
Psalm 73.
25.
Isa.40.1,2
Psal.84.11
ed, no greater *good desired* ; he rai-
fes the *spirit*, comforts the *heart* ;
he is a *Sun* to give *light* unto them,
and a *Shield* to *defend* them ; when
one is brought to that *extremity*, that
not an *Angel*, nor any *creature* can
help; when *friends*, and *means*, and

Psalm.73.
26.
flesh, and *heart*, and *life*, and all do
fail, he ftands by and is the *strength*
of the *heart*, and our *portion* for ever:

Psal.23.1.
Psalm 37.
16.
where *God* is, there no true *comfort*
can be wanting.

Pro. 15.
17,& 17.
1.
    If means, be *little*, he can *bleffe* it,
and make it a *sufficiency*.

1 Kin.17.
14.
Exod. 17.
6.
    If there be no *means*, he can *cre-
ate* it, and caufe a *plenty*.

Exod.16.
4.13,14.
Psal 46.
per totum.
Mat. 4. 4.
Gen. 22.
14.
Micah 7.
8,9,10,11
Haggai 2.
19.
    And in greateft *Exigencies* God
can fo fupply that he can make the
estate of his *Children* as Comfortable as if they had all good things at
hand. *God* will be feen in the *Mount*:
mans extremity is Gods opportunity :
there's no man can be brought to
that defperate *ftate* whom he cannot
eafily

eafily and fpeedily *Recover.*

If *God* be with him, *David* will fear none evil, though he walk in the midft of the valley of the fhadow of *death,* and his own *people* talk of ftoning him. *Peter* can fleep *fecurely* ; and *Paul* fing *fweetly* in the *Prifon,* if *God* be with them. *Daniel* in the *Lyons* den, and the three *Children* in the *fiery Furnace,* are fafe through the *prefence of God.* He proportions his *Confolations* to their *afflictions* : let not then their *hearts* faint, nor their *faith* faile, but when they fit in *darkneffe,* and fee no light, let them truft in the Name of the Lord, and ftay themfelves upon their God, let them not flye to broken *Cifterns,* feeing they have the *fountain* at hand ; and let them not long for ftoln *waters* when they may drink their fill at the *fpring* or *well* of Life. Wherefore ftands *God* by them, but to fill them with his *Grace,* to fupport them in

Hagga. 2.
19.
Pfal 23.4.
1 Sam. 30.
6.
Act. 12.6.
Acts 26.
25.
Dan. 6.22.
Dan. 3.25.
27.
2 Cor. 1.5.
Pf. 94. 19.

Ifa. 50. 10.

Jer. 2. 13.
Jer. 17. 13.
Pfal. 36. 9.
Prov. 9. 17.
Revel. 21.
17.

E   times

times of *danger* and *difficulty?* then *hope* holdeth up the heart ; and *faith*

Isa. 57. 2. assures their *hope,* that eafe, and reft, and peace and deliverance will come:

Pfal. 22. 4, 5. and who ever trufted in *God,* and was difappointed? the confideration hereof made *David* to *check* the difqui-

Pfal. 42 5. 11. etneffe of his *own heart,* and to put it upon *Record* as one of his experimented *Obfervations,* that in all his time

Pfalm. 37. 25. he never faw the Righteous forfaken.

Indeed they may find much *trou-*

Affligeris q idem a-liquandiu; fed fi ad eum redie-ris, te ita profperabit *ble,* feel much fadnefs, be brought to a very *low ebb* : but God will bring them up again : * or if he do not, hec hath *fupplies,* and *fupports* for them.

ut vehe- *menter gaudeas & præ gaudio inrifum folvaris.* Mercerus *in* Job, *cap.* 8.

* Ifa. 60. 14, 15. 16, &c. Deut. 32. 36. 2 Pet. 2. 9. Pf. 51. 8. 12. Pfal. 126. 5, 6. Mark 2. 5. Ifa. 61. 3, & 49. 19. Pfal. 30. 5. Ifa. 55, 11. Ifa. 61. 2. Mat. 5. 4. Joh. 14. 16.

Men

Men see their *sorrows* and *sufferings*; but their *Comforts* and *joyes* men see not, which are such as the *world* knows not of, such as the *world* cannot deprive them of.

Habest intus quo gaudeat. Aug. *in* Ps. 30. *Boni latent, quia totum ipsorum in occulta e'; & tam merita eorum sint: in abscondito constituta q mira e'. rug. sint 201.*

Judg s. 14. 8. 1 Cor 7. 30. Prov. 14. 10. Joh. 16. 10. Luk. 1. 47. Gal. 6. 14. Mat. 5. 12. Psalm 86. 4. 1. Cor. 2. 9 Joh. 16. 22. Isa. 31. 10.

God hath a *bottle* for their *teares*; in all their *afflictions* he is *afflicted*; he is about their *bed*; he putteth under his everlasting *Armes*, and upholdeth them with his *hand* from sinking: their *bodies* may lye in *pain*, but their *souls* shall live at *ease*; and however it fare with them in their outward *estate*, their Soul shall be bound up in the bundle of life with the Lord their God : Nay, he will so *strengthen* them with his *Grace*, arm them with *patience*, *endue* them with *Wisdome*, *protect* them with his

Psal. 56. 8. Psal. 69. 9. Ro. 15. 3. Judges 10. 16 Psal. 41. 3. Deut. 33. 27. Psal. 37. 17. 24. Psal. 57. 1. 1 Sam. 25. 29.

E 2   power

power, and cheer them with his *Spirit*, that neither *paines of death*, nor *powers of hell*, shall be able to *prevaile* against them .

For when the *World* and the *Devil* discover their greatest *malice*, he reveales his greatest *mercies* : the *comforts* of his *love*, the joy of his *presence*, the *light* of his *countenance*, the *blessing* of his *assistance*, found and felt in the *forgivenesse of sins*, in *the testimony of Conscience*, in *the supplyes of his Spirit*, and *assurance of Salvation*, are sufficient to *convince* all accusations of *Men* or *Devils* ; to silence all *murmurings* and *impatience* of our own *hearts*, to heal all *distempers* of *mind*, and to *establish and settle* the Soul in *quietnesse* and *meeknefs.*

For the continuance of sorrow:

To suffer much, and *to suffer long*, is a strong *temptation*, too strong for flesh

flesh to suftain; for one to live many daies, and not fee one good *day*, to begin ones *life* in forrow, and to fee no end of it, is a fad condition ;who can bear it , and not be diftracted ? it was *Davids cafe,*and who of us fhall dwell with everlafting burnings ? (faith the Prophet Ifaiah.)

Pfal.90. 10.
Gen 49.7.
Job. 5.7.
Job 9.25.
Ita fit mi-
feris mors,
fine morte
finis fine
fine, de-
fectus fine
defectu ,

qui1 & mors vivit, & finis femper incipit, & dficere de-
fectus nfcit. Greg. Moral *lib.9.cap.47.*
Pfal.88.5 14. Pfal. 40. 12. Pfal.8. 15. Pfal.77.8,9.Ifa.33.14.

Yet here's the comfort, when God lengthens the day of *Affliction* , he enlarges his *confolation*, and he will never fuffer his *faithfulnefs* to faile , or his *Grace* to forfake thofe who in their *fufferings* feek unto him ; and this is one *comfort* in greateft *tryals*, that if the *affliction* lye very *heavy*, it cannot laft very *long*. The *Win-ter* dayes, they are the *fharpeft*, but they are the *fhorteft* dayes ; the day of *Calamity* begins fadly. Alafs ! for that *day* is great ; none hath been like

John 2. 5.
Pfal.94.13
14.
Pfal.27.10.
Pfal.37 28.
Ifa. 41.17.
Heb.13 5.
Pfal.55. 22.
Pfal.40. 1, 2.
Pfal.50.15,.
Nemo po-
teft valde
dolere &
diu.

E 3
it;

Jer.30.7.　it, it is the day of *Jacobs* trouble ;
Rom.9.28　but *abbreviatum est tempus* ; God in
Pſal.125.　Righteouſneſſe will cut it ſhort ; for
3.　the rod of the Wicked ſhall not reſt
upon the lot of the Righteous. God
doth limit the times of their ſuffe-
Pſal. 39.　rings, they ſhall be but for a little
ult.　while, a little little while, In a little
Iſa.54.8.　wrath I hid my face from them: for a
ſmall moment have I forſaken thee :
Pro brevi　for God is faithfull, and will not ſuf-
bus lachry-　fer his Children to be tempted a-
mis gaudia　bove their ſtrength, but with the
longa me-　temptation will make a way of
tent. Pau-　Evaſion ; and after they have ſuf-
linus No-　fered awhile, make them perfect,
lan. in　eſtabliſh, ſtrengthen, and ſettle them.
Poem.
1 Cor.10.　　　Sometimes God ſetteth down a
13.　*prefixed time* how long the trouble
1 Pet. 5.　ſhall laſt ; the *Jewes Captivity* for ſe-
10.　venty years : *Nebuchadnezzars humi-*
Jer.25.11.　*liation* for ſeven years : *Joſephs impri-*
Dan.4.25　*ſonment* for two years ; the *Tribula-*
Gen.41.　　　　　　　　　　　　　　　　　　*tion*
1.

tion of fome in the *Church* of *Smyrna* for ten dayes; and when the appointed time is come, comes eafe.

For if God fet down a *Day*, hee'l keep his *Word*, and his *time* to a minute ; and therefore let our *forrows* be never fo *great* or fo *grievous*, ftay Gods *leafure*, waite upon his *will* and *pleafure*; be not impatient ; but with all *meeknefs* expect deliverance : and if the vifion ftay, waite for it. It was *Ifaiahs* Refolution, Yet will I wait upon God, though he have hid his face from us. And it was *Davids* Confolation, That he verily believ'd to fee the goodnefs of God in the Land of the living; for the poor fhall not alwayes be forgotten;the patient abiding of the meek fhall not perifh for ever;but *hope* defer'd maketh the heart *fick*, this made *David* think and fay that *God* had quite forgotten him, that he had caft him off for ever,

E 4   that

Rev.2.10.
Pfal. 118.
18.
Pfal.71.20
Luk.24 6.
7.
Prorfus
tanquam
ægrotos
reficiens
medicus ,
& quod o-
pus eft hoc
dat, &
quando o-
pus eft
tunc d:t.
Aug. in
*Pfal.*14 ,
Pfa.27.14
& 31.35.
Heb. 10.
35,36,37.
Hab.2 3.
Ifa 8. 17.
Pfa.2 7.
13.
Pfal.9.18.
Pfal.77 8.
9.

that he should never see good day more.

But he acknowledges his Error, blames his Infirmity and folly thus to *question* the *nature* and *faithfulnes* of God.

Psal 77 10

For *God* is not forgetfull of his *promise*, nor unmindfull of the *sufferings* of his *servants*, if he delay the actual performance of his *promise* and come not in to their *help*, when and how they would have him, they must not *murmure* againſt *God*, nor accuse him of *ſlackeneſs*, or account of what he hath *promiſed* after the manner of *Men*, as if it were only a *promiſe* (that is a verbal *comfort*) without any *purpose* of performance ; for what he *promiſeth* he purpoſeth, and what he *purpoſeth* he will ſurely *performe*.

μέγα κα-
κὸν τὸ μὴ
δύναωθαι
φέρειν κα-
κόν. Laert.

And therefore reſt upon his word and faithfulneſs which will never faile. We muſt not Indent with
God

God : we may not prescribe to him : But leave *him* to his own liberty : he is *free*, though we be *bound*. Let him take his own *time*, and go his own *way* ; he will not be limited : he knows his *time*, and his *time* is the best *time*.

If the *mercy* of God appear not for our Salvation this *day* or the *next*, nor perhaps for many *dayes* to come, wait still, and in its time there shall be an accomplishment of all that is *promised*.

But we are *impatient* ; when we want any *good*, or feele any *pain*, then is our *time* ; but then perhaps is not *Gods time*: we are not yet fit for *mercy*, though he be ever ready to shew it when we are, his *mercy* will appear ; for *mercy* pleaseth him.

When *men* are better'd and a-mended by *afflictions*, their vain *imaginations* cast down, their rebellious *lusts* subdued, their *minds* humbled,

bled,

Psal. 123. 2.
Judith. 9. 15, 16, 17.
Ἐνεργείας
ἐξ τὸ μὴ
σεὶχειρον
ἢ ἐνεργε-
σίας.
Greg. Naz. adversus Eunom.
Psal. 6. 2.
Num. 12.

Micah 7. 18.

bled, their *compassions* towards others stirred up, their *hard hearts* softned, their *affections* weaned from the world : when they search and trye their wayes and *turn* to the Lord, he will then *return* to them ; and if he do not, let them cast themselves down before him with *David*, and say with him, If I shall find favour in the eyes of the Lord, &c. But if he thus say, I have no delight in thee ! Behold here am I ; let him do to me, as it seemeth good unto him.

Patience is a *grace* that pleaseth *God* : let it have its perfect work, and never think of leaving *God*, though he may seem to have left *us*.

God knows our frame and temper, and the metal we are made of : he knows our hard and stubborn *nature* that will never work kindly without the fire. Our hearts are like *steele* and *iron*, easie to be wrought any way, in the *fire* of *affliction*. If this be the, vvay

Acts 3.19.
2 *Chron.*
7.14.

2 *Sam.* 15.
26.
Jam. 1. 4
Isa. 30.18.
Psal. 44.
17,18,19,
20,21.
*Tu, inquit,
avertis
faciem tu-
am à me;
sed ego
non sum a-
versus a te.*
Ruffin. in
Psal. 29.
*Nec ira-
tum colere
destitit
numen.*
*Sen. ad
Marc. cap.*
13.

way he will work us to his *purpose*, let us yield our selves to be wrought upon with *meeknes*; we muſt be content to endure many *heates and blows* untill his work be done; for when that is *finiſhed*, our *ſufferings* ſhall have an end ; or if they have not, but *laſt* as long as life *laſts*, *Chriſtians* muſt be, Phil.2.8. as *Chriſt* was, *obedient unto death*.

Let us not *murmure* againſt *God*, though he ſeem to have left us and to have quite forgotten us : but let us feel our own *pulſes*, and lay our *hands* upon our *hearts*; for doth not *God* deal with *us*, as *we have* dealt with *him*, and pay us in our own *Coine* ? *

Quid eſt quod nos queramur de deo, cum Deus maeis queri de nobis omnibus poſſit? quæ ratio eſt ut doleamus

nos non audiri a Deo, cum ipſi Deum non audiamus ? & ſuſurremus non reſpici a Deo terras, cum ipſi non reſpiciamus ad Cælum; & mol ſtum ſit deſpici a Domino preces noſtras, cum præcepta ejus deſpiciantur a nobis ? quid dignius ? quid juſtius ? non audivimus, non audimur : non reſpeximus, non reſpicimur; quis ergo ex carnalibus dominis hac cum ſuis lege agere contentus eſt ut contemnat tantummodo ſervos ſuos, quia fuerit ab eis ipſe contemptus? Salvianus de Gubern. Dei lib. 3 pag. 85. 86. * Hof. 4. 6. 9.

have

have not we forgotten? have not we neglected? have not we refused? have not we delayed him? what can be more *just and equal*, than that *he* should do by *us* as *we* have done by *him?* *we* are too apt to forget *God* and our selves, when all things go well with *us*: therefore *God* will have it go otherwise, will lay *afflictions* upon *us*, and leave *us* to struggle under the burden, then *we* begin to remember there is a *God,* and that *we* our selves are but *men*; then *we* admire no man, and despise no man : but look up to *God,* and throw down *our selves,* not *fretting or repining,*but with all *meekness* acknowledging that God is Righteous in all his wayes, and holy in all his works.

But what if a man be *alone?* What if he have *none* to bear a part with *him* in his sorrows and sufferings? none to pity *him*, to help *him*, to strengthen *him,*to comfort *him?* this

is

Copia tri-bulationis, inopia con-solationis, quando multifaria is a heavy *cafe.* It was *our Saviours,* for he trod the wine-prefs *alone* ; and when he was ready to be offer'd, all his *Difciples* forfook him and fled. *quis pati-tur, & a nemine relevatur.* Aug. Ifa.63.3. Mark 14. 50.

It was Saint *Pauls cafe,* for he complains that no man ftood with *him* , but all men forfook *him* in his foreft trials. Math.26. 56. 1 Tim. 4. 16.

It was *Davids cafe;* I looked (faith he)on my right hand, and beheld,but there was *no man* that would knovv me ; refuge failed me, *no man* cared for my foul. *Company* is a *comfort* in *calamity,* and two are better than *one* : but wo to him that is *alone;* man could not be happy in *Paradife* vvithout a companion:*God* favv it vvas not good that he fhould be alone (*nullius rei fine focio jucunda eft poffeffio*) hovv heavy then and difcomfortable muft it be,in deepeft forrovvs, and greateft extremities, to have none to *pity* a mans cafe ? all againft *him,* none for Pfal. 142. 4. *Solamen miferis fo-cios habu-iffe doloris.* Ecclef. 4. 9,10. Gen. 2. 18.

him,

John. 4.
32.

*Vobiscum
illic in
carcere
quodam-
modo &
nòs sumus:
separari
dilectio-
nem spiri-
tus non
sinit : vos
illic con-
fessia, me
affectio
includit.*
Cyp. Eph.
16.

John 16.
32.

Psa. 27. 10

2 Tim. 4.
16, 17.
Mat. 1. 23.
Isa 7. 14.

him. Yet here let this be the *Christians
Mo'to,* Bear, forbear, for as our *Saviour*
said to his *disciples,* I have meat to
eat that ye know not of; so *Christians,*
though they seem *alone* in their *sufferings,* have *Comforts and companions*
the World knows not of. You shall
leave me alone (saith Christ to his
Disciples) yet am I not alone, because the Father is with me, so may
the *afflicted Christian :* he is not a-
lone, *God* is with *him, Christ* is with
him, and he is *Emanuel God with us.*
When dearest *friends,* nearest *Rela-
tions,* stand afar off, the *Lord* is at
hand; so *David,* when my Father and
my Mother forsake me, then the
Lord will take me up. So St. *Paul,*
when no man stood with *him,* but
all men forsook *him,* the *Lord,* saith
he, stood with *me,* and strengthened
me. Christ is the Lord, and he is *Emanuel,* God with us.

If the trouble be any *difficulty,* in
matter

matter of duty to be done, he puts his *neck* under the *yoak*, and draws with us, and it becomes *easie*.

Da quod jubes, Domine, & jube quod vis. Aug. Mat. 11. 30. Isa. 53. 4. 7

If it be any *danger*, any *crosse* to be endur'd, he puts his *shoulder* under, helps to bear it, and the *burden* becomes *light*.

Let him never *murmure* at his sufferings, that hath *God* and *Chrift* to bear a part with him that hath the bleffed *Angels* affisting, fupporting, fustaining, and as bleffed *Guardians* preferving him from all evil ; and bearing him in their *armes*, that he dafh not his foot against a ftone; the Angel of the Lord encampeth round about them that fear him, and delivereth them.

Heb. 1. 14 Dan. 10. 19. Pf. 34. 7. Rev. 12. 7. Pfal. 91. 11, 12.

Pfal. 34. 7.

Befides, being in the *Body* every *part* partakes of the priviledge of the *whole* ; and the *members* fhould have the fame care one of another ; as whether one *member* fuffer, all the *members* fuffer with it; for we are called

Quod eft in corpore noftro anima, id eft fpiritus fanctus in corpore chrifti qui

ſi eccleſia. Aug. *Sc.m.*186. *de temp.*

Oculus ſolus vidit in corpore ; ſed nunquid ſoli ſibi oculus videt ? & manui videt, & pedi videt, & cæteris membris videt, Aug. *Tract.* 32. *in Johannem.*

Si enim tauri cum taurum mortuum invenerunt, plorant, mugiunt, & quaſi quibuſdam debitis humanitatis obſequijs fraterna funera proſequuntur : quid debet homo homini, quem ratio docet, & trahit affectio ? ſicut ergo ſanctis animabus invitationem, ſic magis ſanctis compaſſionem debemus, &c. Bern. *Serm. de triplici gen. bonorum. pag.* 382. *col.* 2. F.

If we ſhould ſuppoſe a body to be as high as the

led and commanded to bear one anothers *burdens*; there is in the body a *Sympathy* becauſe there is a neer Conjunction of *members* in one *body*, and of the *body* with one *head* ; nor can the diſtance of *place* diſſolve or break off that *Union* which the *members* have in the *body*, or the *body* with the *head*, for although the *head* be in Heaven, and the *body* upon Earth ; although one *member* be in *England*, and another in *India*, yet the whole *body* being mo-

Heavens, that the head thereof ſhould be where Chriſt our head is, and the feet where we his members are : no ſooner could that head think of moving one of the toes, but inſtantly the thing would be done, without any impediment given by that huge diſtance of the one from the other, and why ? becauſe the ſame ſoul that is in the head, as in the fountain of ſence and motion, is preſent likevviſe in the loweſt member of the body. *Uſher Archiep. Armach. in Serm. coram Dom. Com. apud Weſt.* Feb. 18. 16.20. *in* 1 Cor. 10. 17.

                                            ved

influence of one
ated and acted
the same *spirit*,
:ame to pass that
and noblest *part*
f the hurt and
ie meanest and
. He then that
dy cannot com-
lone ; seeing *God*
l the *Son* of God;
t of God; and the
God ; and the
God: all the
God stand by
o' he hath many
for him : many
rk for him : ma-
to intercede for
aring a part with
gh to *quiet him* ,
iis *complaints*, and
know he suffers

In toto universali, quic-
quid totius est, etiam
partis est. Log. Max.
Ecce spinam calcat
pes : quid tam longe
ab oculis quam pes?
longe est loco, proximè
est charitatis affectu.
Lingua dicit, quid me
calcas, non ipsa cal-
cata est, calcas me
charitas dicit. Aug.
Tract. in 1. Jo. *mag-*
num profecto habituri
sunt testimonium quos
in cælo pater susceper-
rit tanquam filios &
hæredes, filius asci-
verit tanquam fratres
& cohæredes, spiritus
sanctus adhærentes
Deo unum spiritum
faciat esse cum eo. Est
enim spiritus ipse in-
dissolubile vinculum
trinitatis per quem si-
cut pater & filius u-
num sunt, sic & nos u-
num sumus in ipsis.
Bern. mort. Pasch. ser.
1. *de tribus testimo-*
niis in cælo & in ter-
ra pag. 189. Col. 1. *in*

s orbis comunione firmamur. Aug. de unit. Ec. c. 2.

F

But in another *case*, *meeknes* is
sore affaulted, when one *suffers* what
no man elfe doth.   To be in *trouble*
when all others are *quiet*: to lie in
pain when others live at *eafe*, to be
in want when others have what they

Pfa. 12.8.
Job.24.24
Eccl.7.7.
Deut.27.
25.
Pfal.10.8.

can defire.   To fee *wickednes* ex-
alted & *innocency* opprefled: oppref-
fion (faith *Salomon*) will make a
wife man mad.   But if God, *will*
have it fo, there is no *remedy* but
meeknes.

God deals with his *Children* as the
Embroiderer with his *cloath* of gold
and other rich ftuffes; cuts them
into many *peeces*, laies them confu-
fedly on an *heap*, until he refume
them to make up his *imagery*.   So

ἄλλος μὲν
δ᾽ ἀλλο τῆ
τῶν πα-

God firft cuts in *peeces* his *children*
with *croffes and afflictions*, but fets

λαιῶν ἤ τ νέων κατωρθωκέναι πιςεῖεται ὡς ἕκαςος ἐ τυχειν
ἐκ θεῦ χάριτος τιν᾽ ἠξιωμέν᾽. Ἰα᾽ 6 τὸ ἐν τοῖς πάθεσι καρτε-
ρικόν κ᾽ ἀγάλωτον. Μωϋσῆς κ᾽ Δαβὶδ τὸ πρᾷον Σαμυελ το
χρηματισαι, βλέπωντα τῆ ἔμπροθεν. Greg. Naz. Orat. 19.

them

them together again in excellent *forms*, to be look'd upon as *examples* to the *world*, thus he dealt with *Abraham*, with *Moses*, and with *Job*; that he might preferve them, and prefent them as *patterns* of *obedience*, *meeknefs*, and *patience*; to all fuccee-ding *ages*.   Now if we confier what God does to *particulars*, we may perhaps find juft matter of *complaint*,

Gen. 12.
Exod. 2.
Job. 1.
Job. 2. 7, 8.

Quæritur itaque, cum hæc ita fint, fi totum judicio Dei

quod in hoc mundo eft; cura & gubernaculo & agitur; cur melior multo fit Barbarorum conditio quam noftra? cur inter nos quoque ipfos fors bonorum durior quam malorum: cur probi jaceant, improbi convalefcant? poffim quidem rationabiliter & fatis conftanter dicere: nefcio fecretum, & confilium divinitatis ignoro, &c. Sufficiat tibi quod Deus a fe agi ac difpenfari cuncta teftatur. Quid me interrogas, quare alter major fit alter minor? alter mifer alter beatus? alter fortis, alter infirmus? qua caufa quidem hæc Deus faciat non intelligo; fed ad pleniffimam rationem abunde fufficit, quod a Deo agi ifta demonftro; ficut enim plus eft Deus quam omnis humana ratio: fic plus mihi debet effe quam ratio, quod a Deo agi cuncta cognofco. Nihil ergo in hac re opus eft, novum aliquid audiri, fatis fit pro univerfis rationibus autor Deus. Salvianus de Guber. Dei lib. 3. ab Initio.

and

Genu-
inus ergo
Chriſti
diſcipulus
non ſibi
præſumit
ſcrupuloſe
Deo præ-
ſcribendi
quid &
quantum
ſibi impo-
nere, aut
quomodo
ſecum age-
re debeat.
Neque e-
tiam ſub

&think there is *diſorder* and *injuſtice* in the works of God, but whenl we lay them all together weſhal find the compoſition excellent, and of ſingular uſe and benefit to us. And that God *doth not*, nor permitteth any thing to *be done* unto the *righteous* but only for their *good.* And therefore to *murmure or repine* againſt God, or to *queſtion* why he affl cts one man more than another, were in effect to *queſtion* why he loves one man more than another.

cruce conſtitutus, oculos curioſe ad alios convertit, & cum Petro *dicit, quid autem hic multo minus impatienter, queritatur quaſi Deus aliis breviora ſibi autem graviora & difficiliora portanda impoſuerit. Sed in bona Dei voluntate patienter acquieſcit, certus Deum optime omnium noviſſe quid ipſi ad refrænandam carnem laſcivientem ſit maxime conducibile,* &c. Kemnitius. Har. Evang. cap. 86. pag. 1647. col. 1.

But what if the cauſe of trouble be the *conſciouſneſs* of ſome known *ſin* with the apprehenſion of Gods juſt

juſt *anger,* when a man ſees *God* ſet
againſt him, and his own *conſcience*
againſt him : *Gods anger* and a *woun-*
ded ſpirit who can bear ?

When the *ſpirit* is overwhelmed
with grief and fear, it drives a man
out of his right mind, which in its
diſtemper apprehends nothing but
bitterneſs : the bed of *eaſe* is a *tor-*
ment, where dreams do ſcare, and
viſions terrefie, ſo that the ſoul chu-
ſeth ſtrangling and death rather then
life.*Job.*7.14,15.

This trouble *David* felt in a great
meaſure : which made him complain there was no ſoundneſs in his
fleſh : no reſt in his bones : no *quiet*
in his *mind* : no *comfort* in his *ſoul :*
the *ſight* of his *ſins,* and *ſence* of Gods
anger, had ſo diſtracted him, that he
roared for the very diſquietneſs of
his heart.

In this caſe take *meekneſs ;* and
this will bear *up* and bear *out* the ſpi-

Job.7.3,4
Job.7.13,
14,15,16

Pſal.38.3

Pſ.38.4.

Pſa.38. 8.

rit

rit, and beware by any means of saying as *Cain* said, mine iniquity is
Gen. 4.13 greater then can be forgiven; (*my
punishment greater then I can bear.*)

Jer. 10.19
Mic 7. 9.
1 Joh. 1.7
2 Cor. 12.
9.
Mat. 20.
23.30
1 Joh 1. 9
Eph. 2 4.
Jo. 3. 16.
Isa. 25.8.
Ps. 52. 1.
Psa. 86. 5.
Ro. 11. 22
Psa. 33. 5.
Ps. 100. 5.
Ps. 145 9.
Psa. 34. 8.
Psal. 103.
8,9,13.
Rom. 2. 4. But pluck up thy heart, and say
with *Jeremiah, This is my sorrow
and I will bear it.* And with the
Prophet *Micah, I will bear the indig-
nation of the Lord, because I have sin-
ned against him.*

And in this *case* there is no cause
of too much *dejection and distemper.*
For if we consider,

The excellency of the *merits* of
Christ: the sufficiency of his *grace*:
the wisdom of Gods *providence*: the
faithfulnes of his *promises*: how
rich he is in *mercy*: how infinite in
love: and that his goodnes neither
is nor can be exceeded by any wret-
chednes or sinfulnes of *man.*

He is so *patient,* that he is long ere
he be provoked; and when he is
provoked, he is so *gracious,* that he
is

is eafie to be appeafed: men cannot fo foon fall out with their *fins*,
though they have grievoufly *offended :* but he fals in with them, and
becomes gracioufly *reconciled.*

And as a compaffionate and an in-
dulgent *Father* forfakes not his *Child*
when he is *fick*, fo neither will *God*
leave his *Children* when they have
finned ; *He* may take *diftaft* : *they*
may be *dejected* (but being his) his
grace and their *faith* fhall never fail.

Ifa.57. 19
17,18.
Num.14.
18.
Exod. 34.
6,7.
Ez.18.21,
22,23.
Ez.18.31,
32.
Mat.11.
28.
1Tim.1.15.
Mat.1.21.
Ifa.49.15.
Pfal.327,
Pf.89.30.
Pf.51.

Pf.37.24. Mat.24.24.Rom.5.20 1 Joh 5.9. Jam.2 17 Rom.
11.1.Mal.3.6.Rom.11.29.1 Joh.4.4. Jer.32.40. 2 Tim.4 .18.
Deus non deferit etiamfi deferere videatur Aug.in Pf.44 *Delicta
non videt vis amoris.*Chryfologus *Serm.3.de filio prodigo.*

By fuch erroneous fins they greatly off.nd God, incur
the guilt of death, greive the holy fpirit, break off the exercife
of faith, moft grievoufly wound the confcience, now and then
for a time loofe the fenfe of grace, until upon their returning
into the way by true and earneft repentance Gods Fatherly
countenance fhine again upon them. The judgment of the
Synod of *Dort. de quinque Art. controv.in Ecclef.* Belg. *cap.*5.
de perfev. Sanct. Sect. 5.

As in Peter and David 2 Sam.13. Luk. 22. See it in *Ori-
gen,* and others in primitive times. *Putas hic eft, non poteft
non effe,fed latet.*Hyems eft; *intus eft viriditas in radice.*Aug.
in Joh.9.*Habitus non amittitur: actus intermittitur: gradus
remittitur.Vide*Aug.in lib. de correp.& gra.   F 4   For

Pſ. 42. 5. 11
Pſ. 38. 6.
Mat. 13. 4,
5, 6, 7.
Rev. 2 4.
Pſ. 51. 12.
2 Tim. 2.
19.
Rom. 11. 5.
1 Jo. 3. 9.
Heb. 6. 10.
Pſa. 55. 22
2 Tim. 2.
13.
Pſa. 34. 8.
Joh. 6. 47.
Mal. 3. 6.
Pſ 10. 2,
27.
Heb. 13. 8.
Iſa. 59. 1.
2 Tim. 2.
12.
Jo. 10.
28, 29.

For although the *exercise* and former comforts of *grace* may be leſſened : the good *motions* of the *ſpirit* ſuppreſſed : the wonted *fervour* of it abated : and the ſenſible *operation* of it interrupted : yet ſtill *it is there*, when it is not felt : *they have it* though they know not of it. For it cannot be , God ſhould *forget*, though man may be *forgetful*; God cannot *deny* himſelf ; nor will he *deny* his favour to them that come unto him for it : what *God* hath *been* he *is* ſtill : and can *do*, as much as he hath *done*: He will not leave the *claim* where he hath taken poſſeſſion ; *reject* what he hath *receiv'd*: nor *diſclaim* what he hath once *own'd*: He

Joh 13. 1. 1 Pet. 1. 4, 5. Pſa. 89. 35. Luk. 22 32. Eph 4. 3.

For God who is rich in mercy according to unchangeable purpoſe of election, doth not wholly take away his holy ſpirit from his, no not in their grievous ſlips, nor ſuffers them to wander ſo far as to fall away from the grace of adoption & ſtate of juſtification, or to comit the ſin unto death, or againſt the holy Ghoſt, or to be altogether forſaken of him. *Judicium.* *Syn. Dodr. de 5. Art. Controv. in Eccl. Belg. c. 5. de perſev. Sect. 6.*

will

will not fuffer his *truth* to fail ; nor his *fpirit* to forfake the *heart*, into which it hath been once admitted.

When doubts are raifed concerning things *promifed* let them call to mind what they have known *performed*, and let this affure them of *receiving* more. It were extream *weaknefs* for men to forfake their own *ftedfaftnefs*, and overwhelmed with the *waves* of temptation and corruption, to leave their hold of that which can only keep them from *finking*. **2 Pet. 3. 17**

Let the *temptations* of *Sathan* be never fo ftrong : the corruption of their ovvn hearts never fo *great*; their fins never fo *many* ; yet the *mercies* of God, and the *merits* of *Chrift* applied to the contrite *fpirit*, the humbled *foul* : the believing *heart* by the foveraign and healing hand of divine *Grace* doth over-povvre all that can be oppofed ; vvhofe operations can-

not

not either by *Satans* subtlety, or *mans* frailty be frustrated or hindred, for so long as there is *power* in God to make him *able*: and *goodnes* in God vvhich vvill make him *willing* to help and ease the *afflicted* (for vvho is a God like unto him, forgiving iniquity, transgression, and sin) *fall* they may :

Mic.7 18.
utterly *fall away* they cannot, for the
Psa.37.24
Lord upholds them vvith his hand; though some be of *tender hearts* apt to entertain troublesome *fears* and to have a hard *opinion* of themselves : yet let them not *Judge* amiss of God vvho hath *mercy* laid up for all that vvill seek it. God saith not to the humbled *sinner* as Christ said to the *Jews* (you shall dye in your sins) but as he said to the *sisters of Laza-*

Joh. 8.21.
rus, of Lazarus sicknesse, this *sicknes*

Joh. 11.4.
(this sin) is not unto *death.* Sin is the sickness of the soul, the *Soul* may be far spent vvith *sin* as the *body* vvith

Isa. 66.2.
Isa. 61.1.
Isa. 35.3.
sicknes : but though the humors be corrupted

corrupted and the *bloud* diftempered : yet if *nature* be not quite exhaufted, and the *fpirits of life* extinguifhed, the *fkilfull Phyfitian* hath hope to cure the body.

In like manner the *foul Phyfitian* will bind up the broken *heart* : quiet the troubled *fpirit* : cherifh the feeds of *grace* : forgive the *fins* of the *foul* ; and reftore to a finner the joy of his *falvation.* If they have *faith* to believe the promifes of *God*, and *repentance* to bewaile their fins : God hath *mercy* to *heal* their *fouls*: the *medicine* and *means* of recovery is neither *weak* nor *wanting* to him that can *apply* it.

If Sa'an put a *conceit* into the *head* of the finner; that *God* will not be entreated : let it not get the *confent* of the *heart.*

To *fin* is *dangerous* ; but to caft away all *hope* of forgivenefs is *defperate,* and therefore give not way to

4.5.6 .
If. 61.2.3.
Ro.8.26.
Io.4.3.4.
Mat.12.20.
Ifa.37.15
Joh.14.18
Ifa. 42. 3.--
Ifa. 55.12
Mat. 9. 2.
Col.1.13.
Ifa.53.1.
Ifa.65 18
Chryfoft.
in Gen.
*Ham.*19.
Pf 51.12.
Pf.22.14,
15,17,24.
1Tim 4.10
1Tim.2. 4.
Jo.11.25.
Act.3.19.
Joel.2.12
2 Pet.3.9 .
Ifa.55. 7
Lu.24.49
Ez.33.11
Ifa.1. 18.
Ifa.43.25,
Jer.3.1,22
13,22.

1Tim.2.4.Pf.103.10,11,12.1Kin.8.45 &c.Rom.5.15,16, 17,&c.
*Vch m n'er & fupra omnem modum exuperat gratia Dei delicto-rum magnitud'nem, copiam & gravitatem.*Laur Alex. *pag.*95 .

1 Cor. 15. 56
Ro. 6. 23.
Ez. 18. 20.
Lu. 13. 3.
Ja. 1. 15.
Eph. 5. 6.
Pf. 31. 22.
Job. 33. 10

Omne peccatum grave eſt.
Greg. ſup Ez. li. 2.
For every ſin muſt be accounted for.

Mat. 12. 36

* *Plut. in vita Demoſthenis.*

Merito perit ægrotus qui medicum non vocat, ſed ultro qui venientem reſpuit.
Muſculus.

Heb. 10. 35
Job. 13. 15
Heb. 3. 12
1 The. 5. 8.
Dan. 9. 9.

your own *corruptions*, and Satans *temptations* : if you be *weak*, yet in any caſe be not *wilfull*; and take heed that a ſin of *infirmity*, become not a fall of *Apoſtacy*. It is the *Apoſtles* advice , caſt not away your confidence, but keep your hold ſtill : which *Job* would not forgoe, though God kill'd him.   It is an evil heart, and unfaithfull, that thinks of departing from the living *God*.   *Chriſtians* in their *conflicts* muſt not do as * *Demoſthenes* did in the *battel*, caſt away their *ſhield* (*the hope of ſalvation*,) for God hath not loſt the *bowels* of *compaſſion* , if men have not loſt all *ſence* of *grace*.   There is no *ſin* ſo great : but is pardon'd to the *penitent* : if man have the *power* to *repent* : God hath a *will* to *forgive*, his *hand* is never *ſhortned*, but when mens *hearts* are *hardned*.

Think of *Manaſſes* Idolatry : *Davids* adultery : *Noahs* drunkenneſs:
Peters

Peters denial, and *Pauls* blaſphemy ,
all theſe *ſinned* greatly but being
greatly *humbled* for their ſins by
prayer and true *repentance* they ob-
tained *pardon* : they could plead nothing but *mercy*;and this may any one
plead as well as they, and therefore
never *murmure* at God, or *repine* at
thine own condition : but be contented,and thankfull,and *put on meek-
neſſ* : Repent and be converted, and
a time of refreſhing will come.

    But *nature* is a great enemy to this
excellent *grace*,for the *nature* of ſome
is peeviſh and tachie, and content
in no *condition* ; *never well either full
or faſting* (as we uſe to ſay.)

    Some when they have what they
can *deſire*, yet enlarge their *deſires* as
hell ; and *grudge* if they be not *ſa-
tisfied* : they *murmure* under *plenty*,
and whereas *neceſſaries* ſhould ſuffice,
they are not content with *ſuperflu-
ities*,It is not enough that their *cove-
touſneſs*

Hab. 2. 5.
Pſa. 5.15.
1 Tim. 6.
7, 8.
Nam ideo
*fines tran-
ſilimus,
quia ad
mille vi-
tas,quas
falſa ima-
gine con-
cipimus,
ſolicitudo
noſtra ſe
extendit—
unuſquiſ-
que votis
immenſa
latifundia
non ſecus
abſorbet,
quam ſi al-
vum habe-
ret dimidiū
mundi (ca-
pacem.*
Calv.in 1
Tim.5.7.

tousness is answer'd with *plenty* : but their *curiosity* longs after *novelty* ; and if the multiplied *devices* of a luxurious wanton *age*, do not present themselves to their longing *appetites*: if their *dyet* be not some choice *delicacy* ; and their *apparrel* of the costliest *stuff* and newest *cut and fashion* : they are *sick* of the *sullens*, and out of *charity* : both with *God* and *man*, such *Humorists* were the *Israelites* who *murmured* against *God*, untill he *corrected* their corrupt *humors* by slaying the *wealthiest* of them in the *wildernesse*.

Some again are *troubled,* and they

Quum a-limenta & vestiarium nominat, delicias & abundantem copiam ex-cludit. Calv. in 1 Tim. 5. 8.

Prodiga rerum luxuries nunquam parvo contenta paratu: & quæsitorum terra pelagoque ciborum ambitiosa fames, & lautæ gloria mensæ. Lucan. lib. 4. de bel. civil.

In Coccino & Tyrio, &c. cedo acum crinibus distinguendis, & pulverem dentibus elimandis, & bisulcum aliquid ferri vel æris unguibus repastinandis: si quid ficti nitoris, si quid coacti ruboris, in labia aut genas urgeat, &c. Tert. lib. de Pænit. cap. 11.   Psal. 78. 31. Num. 11. 33.

know

know not *where*, nor know not *why*, but *diſcontent* they are, and out of all *patience,complain* of croſſes,and loſſes, and wants, of diſappo'ntments and pains, when they cannot tell where the pain *holds* them.

In this *caſe* take heed there be not ſome *Canaanite*, ſome *Jebuſite* in the Land, ſome ſecret *ſin* in the ſoul Joſ.23.13. unrepented of; which (as a ſcourge in the ſide, and a thorne in the eye) will ſuffer a man to take no *Reſt*.

. Moreover, ſome are naturally *ſad*, *penſive* and *melancholy*, fall out with *themſelves*, repine againſt *God*, and every *man* ,they abandon all *comfort*, and repell all *occaſions* of joy, delighting to nouriſh *grief* , and to entertain a *penſive* ſoul, they *eate* up their own *hearts*, and *drink* up their own *ſpirits*, this is a dangerous (I had almoſt ſaid) a devilliſh *humor* (one hath ſaid it) *Spiritus melancholicus eſt ſpiritus Diabolicus*, the *Devil* loves

to fish in troubled *waters,* and is the most discontented *spirit* in the World.

Discontent is oft *desperate: Sathan* hath a Cord, a knife, &c. *Hang: drowne: stab:* a violent *hand,* a virulent *tongue* are his *Instruments* to destroy *man* and blaspheme *God,* they are *impatient* of all *pain*: the least *crofs* overwhelmes them ; and so affects them ; that they *know not*: they *care not* what they say or do, they *Quarrel* with *God,* with themselves, and with all *men;* a sad condition, and enemy to *meeknefs.* But all this while I have not clear'd the *Saints* of that *scandal* that is taken against them for their distempered *behaviour* in their *afflictions. Jobs* uncharitable *friends* in effect tell him to his *face* (that he rav'd and talk'd idlely,) That the *Saints* have transgreff'd in their *fits,* cannot be deni'd, they were men of like *paffions* with us, and in their *paffions*

Job.1 1 2.
& 8.2.
Job.15.2,
3.
Job.35.16
Act.14.15
Jam.5.17

sions sometimes mutin'd against *God*, and in the *weakness* of their *spirits* did shrink under the *cross*. *Jacob* for the loss of a Son will go down into the *grave* sorrowing : *Moses* speaks unadvisedly with his *lips* : *Jonas* frets, and is *angry* : *Elias* is weary of his *life* ; and *Job* expostulates and reasons with *God*, and thinks him too *severe* : and in this they were carnal (as St. *Paul* speaks) walkt as men by *sense*, and not by *faith* : but *reason* corrects *sense* : and *faith* rectifies *reason* : and when they come to their right *reason*, they acknowledge with *David*, it was their *infirmity.* It is sure the *Saints* of God have a *body* of flesh, as well as a spiritual *soul* : their *flesh* is sensible and their *souls* affectionate ; and as the one is *sensible* of the pain, so the other is *moved* with it ; indeed to be more affected than there is *cause* is *sinfull* : and it is sinfull not to be affected, where *cause* is given. G And

Gen. 37.
35.
Psal. 106.
33.
Jonah 4.1
1 Kin. 19.
4.
Job. 10. 20
Job. 13 25
26, 27.
1 Cor. 3:
1, 3, 4.

Psl. 77. 10.

And if the *Saints* have been much affected under the *Crosse* : they are therein not to be excus'd only but *justified* : if from a just ground for sin *committed*, and God *offended*. To apprehend *God offended*, and angry : and angry he will not be but for sin : and for this we find the *Saints* to have been both strangely and strongly *affected*, read the *Psalms* of David, the *Lamentations* of Hieremy, and see what impression the effects of Gods *anger* did make upon their *affections*; and this *God* not only approv'd : but commanded, and *blames* them when they were not as was meet *affected* at his smiting them.

He layes a *Charge* on them to *rend* their hearts, to *afflict* their souls, to *put* on *sack-cloth* : to *sit in* ashes : to *sigh and cry* : to *weep and mourn* : and to make other *deep expressions* of troubled affections even to *indignation* and *revenge* (two main parts of
.Repentance

Margin notes:
Iob 7 21.
Jona. 3.8.
10.
Joel 2.12.
17.
Isa.9.13.
Jer.2 30.
Jer.5. 3.
Jer. 6.26.
2 Cor. 7.
11.
Let *Tert.* speak the discipline of Primitive Christians.
Nos vero jejuniis aridi, et omni continentia expressi, ab omni vitæ fruge dilati, in sacco & cinere volutantes invidia.

Repentance as *Saint Paul* fets it forth) for *God* will have them break their *fpirits* : humble their *fouls* : be angry with, and take *revenge* of themfelves by the wholfome *difcipline* of fpiritual *mortification.*

Thus to do in dear *affection* , and true *devotion* unto God, unfained *contrition* for their fins : and *compaffion* towards man may well confift with that *meeknefs* which the Apoftle requireth to be *put on.*

But here two *extreams* muft be avoided, a *mean* muft be obferved : and it is a bleffed *thing* to hit it, to know both *when* to be affected and *how far.*

Affections of themfelves are apt enough to run into *excefs,* have more need of the *curb* than the *fpur,* Saint *Paul* fpeaking of the *Apoftles* and their *fufferings,* fayes, they were made as *gazing-ftocks,* a *fpectacle* to the world and to Angels and to men, fuch

G 2   are

Cælum tendimus, &c.
Tert. Apol. adverf. gent. cap. 40 in fine *p. 71.*
Pfa 51. 17
1 Pet. 5. 6.
Gal. 5. 24.
Col. 3. 5.
Rom. 8. 13
1 Cor. 9. 27.
Ne frena animo permitte calenti. Stat. 8. Theb.
imperat hunc frenis, hunc tu compefce catena.
Hor. ep. lib. 1. ep. 2.
Pone iræ frena modũ que. Horat. Satyr 8
Heb. 13. 33
1 Cor. 4. 9.

are the *Saints* they have many *eyes* upon them, and therefore should have a *care* to comport themselves decently and exemplarily that no *pains or passions* difcompofe or disorder the decencie of their *thoughts or duties*. It may be, by their *sufferings* God intends the *instruction* of others: and it is a heavenly thing, when others as well as themfelves, are better'd by their *afflictions*.

To do otherwife were to *fall short* of their duty, or to *exceed* it, *they fall short* of their duty, that being afflicted are not *humbled*: not *senfible* of Gods anger, nor *moved* with it.

This fome would bear the world in hand is their *Patience, Meeknefs* and *Calmenefs* of fpirit: but indeed it is a *stoical negligence* and *carelefsnefs*, a *fencelefs dulneffe and stupidity*.

When Gods hand is lifted up they will not *fee*; they will not *grieve*, nor Ifa.26.11. *fear*, nor be *humbled*, nor *troubled*, not
daunted

daunted or *dejected :* there is no man
but would diſlike that in his *Child,*
and repute it *ſtubbornneſs* rather than
meekneſs and ſo will God, who is
greatly *afflicted* when he ſees *affliction* has no kindly work upon
men.

For *men* to be *affected* and paſſionate to be moved and troubled at the
effects of Gods *anger* may ſtand
both with *Reaſon* and *Grace.*

To this end God hath given man
a ſoft and flexible *nature* to take impreſſion of every *paſſion,*So that when
God is *angry* he will have us to pour
out our ſupplications and complaints
to lament after him, and to be very
much diſpleaſed with our ſelves,
that judging of our ſelves , we may
not be judged of the Lord.

They *exceed* their duty that in their
afflictions are too much troubled, our
nature urgeth downwards, and our
paſſions have their ſelf aptneſs and

Pſal.142.
2.
Jer. 4.8.
1 Cor.11.
31.

G 3   proneſs

Gen 6.5.
& 8. 21.
pronesse to that which is *evill*, *men* o-
therwise *unblameable*, herein are
worthy to be *blam'd* ; that any little
or light *affliction* doth too much *disquiet* them, and makes them wondrous *impatient*, yea many for a small
loss do so *vex* and *fret*, that like Ra-
Jer.31.15 *chel* they refuse to be *comforted*, and
become so *peevish* that no good *counsel* can *charme* them to *patience*, like
Jon. 4.9. *Jonah* they will defend their *frowardnesse*, and with him will tell you
they do well to be *angry*, but as God
to him so I may say to them, do you
well to be *angry* for a trifle ? what is
this or that man ? or what is any
man ? that he should be so *tender* and
tachie, there are very *few* that can be
found better than *David*, or if than
David better than *Christ*, I am sure
they cannot be, yet *David* in the person of *Christ* saies of himself (I am a
Psa.22.6. worm and no man) the best man
compared with God is but as a *worm*
of the earth.   If

If then God shall *tread* upon us shall we turn against him : if he shall *set* against us : shall we *strive* against him! no! rather let us *submit* unto him, and *humble* our selves before him, adoring his *wisedome*, and admiring the unsearchableness of his *wayes* who ordereth all things if against our *wills* : yet according to *his own*.

Yet there are some that shoot their *arrows* against heaven even bitter *words*, fearfull execrations, heavy curses, reviling God and Man if they be cross'd in their designs, and all things answer not their *desires*, they break out into exclamations and accusations against God, and in their furious and frantick *fits* with great horror they utter such prodigious *speeches* that are inconsistent altogether with *Christianity or humanity*, they forget themselves to be *Christians*, to be *men*, and behave themselves as *brutes and devils*, ready to

Atque Deos atque astra vocat crudelia mater. Virg. Eclog. 5.

for-

forſake *God,* to revolt from *Religion,*
full of bitter *thoughts,* breaking
forth into ſuch horrid *expreſſions,*
which will make the heart of any
moderate man to *quake and tremble*
for to hear them in the heighth of
their *madneß,* raging againſt God and
his creatures. Good men under
the ſenſe and pain of ſome heavy
afflictien, may be affected, may be
moved, but affected or moved above
meaſure they may not be, *rayling,* and
reviling, curſing and blaſpheming is
the language of *Hell,* and that man
that uſes it, is no better than an in-
carnate *Devil,* a paſſion to be tamed,
and with much caution, as a dangerous *pitfall* to be ſhunned ; and begge
of God an *humble,* and a *meek ſpirit,*
and thus much for *meekneß* as it re-
lates to *God.*

The

*The second kind of meekneß which re-
lates to man.*

Of *Meekneß* towards *Man.*

Meekneß towards *men* is ſhewn in
a kind *affection*, and in a ſweet and
gentle *converſation*, and is chiefly
intended in this place.

And this kind of *meekneß*, which
the *Apoſtle* here commends to be
put on, is a *calmneſs* of ſpirit, a *quietneſs* of mind, a *gentle moderation* in
all our actions. When as the ſwel-
ling of *anger* together with the *vexa-
tions* and *diſquietneſs* of heart and
mind are ſuppreſt, when as both an
internal and external *tranquillity* is
obſerved, with *modeſty* of countenance, together with a ſweet and
amiable *comportment* of the whole
body, whoſe *tongue* is the law of
kindneſs, with *words* both *few* and
ſoft

The Cha-
racter of
meekneſs
towards
men.

ſoft; affable ; and courteous : *cenſo-rious* of none, *injurious* to none, *re-ſpective* of all ; patient, mild, and hum-ble : ever ready to give a *reaſon* of the hope that is in you to any one that ſhal move the queſtion, & to give the beſt *conſtruction* of every action that *charity* will bear. For *meekneſs* like *charity hopeth* all things: *believeth* all things: *endureth* all things : & is ſo far from *doing* evil, that it *thinks* none.

    Meekneſs of all others knows how to make a *vertue* of neceſſity, and to put evil to good uſe. It cannot be *diſcountenanc'd*, will not be *diſcontent*, hath learn'd to paſs by *Indignites*, to put up *injuries*: *praies* for what it cannot *help*: *laments* what it cannot *mend*: and patiently *ſuffers* what it abhorres to *do*: bearing *wrongs*, and forbearing *revenge*: receiving *evil*, but returning *good*: *good* for *evil*: for *hatred, love*: for *blows, bleſsings.*

    Thus God as the perfection of
                  our

1 Cor. 13.
7.
Rom. 13.
10.

Rom. 12.
19.
Mat. 5. 44.

our *meekness* requires at our hands
not only a free *remission* of all *injuries*
that we forgive men their trespasses:
but also an entire *affection* to their
persons, to love even our enemies.

To recompence to no man evil
for evil is a fair measure of *meekness*,
but to *overcome* evil with good is a
very high degree of *Meekneffe*,
and such as well becomes *Christians*,
who are the followers of that **Master**
who shed his *blood* for them that spilt
it.

You hear what *meekness* is the *vertue* here commended: now will you
hear what *use* we are to make of it,
it must be *put on*.

Put on *meekness*.

Meekness is a *garment* or apparel
for the soul: and as a man is seen in
his *clothes*, and known by them: so
is a *Christian* by *meekness*. This
meekness it comes not by *nature*; it
is a *grace* of God, a *fruit* of the spirit.
And

Mat. 6. 14.

Mat. 5. 44.
Rom. 12.
17.
Luk. 6. 27,
28.
Rom. 12.
21.

And a man may as well be said to be born with *clothes* on his back as with *grace* in his heart.

This and all other *graces* we have not only as the *gift* of God to us: but as the *work* of God in us.

Jam. 1. 7.
1 Cor. 15. 10.
Gal. 2 9.
Eph 4. 7.
Rom. 12. 3. & : 5.

It is a spiritual and heavenly *garment*, and suited to the soul.

It is a wonder to see what a great deal of *care* there is to get *apparel* for the body; and *curiosity* to fit it, that it may be *comly*; what strange *attires* for *fashion*. and unreasonable for *charge*, are devised and worn beyond ability. But the best and seemliest *garment* (which is *meeknes*) is not regarded.

This *Garment* the Apostle adviseth to get, and not to *get* it only,

Ornemus nofmetipfos Spiritualibus ornamentis &c. hac funt veftimenta quibus placere poterimus Jefu Chrifto cœlefti fponfo. Bern. *lib. de modo bene vivendi. Serm. 9. de habitu. pag.* 1251

Ita me Chriftus benè amet, pudere nos hujus noftra detestanda luxuria, intus & in corde noftro debebat; qua indubitatum vaniffime mentis noftra eft Τεκμήριον. *Dietericus. in Antilog. Evang. Domini. in Domin. 1. Trin. par. 1. doct. 3.*

but

but to *wear* it. It is a fearful thing to think of the great neglect of this *Apparel.* But for that of the body what a deal of time is taken up (as they say) between the *comb and the glass.* What care about the back? what dreffing, and tricking, and trimming, and fo many trifles go to the compleating of a *fuit*; that a *fhip* is as eafily *rig'd* as a *woman arrai'd.* *Appelles* his *Prentice* about to draw the face of *Hellen,* failing in his *skill,* painted her *rich* : much like to thofe who when they fail of *vertue* to beautifie their *lives,* think to be known by their fine *clothes.* A many *fuites* for their backs, and never a *grace* for their hearts: furely thofe are

Plus gaudeas intus in anima de fanctis virtutibus quam foris in corpore de pretiofis veftibus. Bern. in lib. de modo bene vivendi. Serm. 9. de habit. O adolefcens cum non poffis pingere pulchram, pinxifti divitem. Clem. Alex.3.

Non eft fine macula Chrifti fponfa, fi amat veftem pretiofam. Bern. *de modo bene vivendi Serm. 9. de habitu.*

Soror in Chrifto amabilis, divitiæ tuæ fint boni mores: pulchritudo tua fit bona vita. Bern. *in lib. de modo bene vivendi. Serm.9. de habitu. pag.* 1251.

Veftes enim noftræ virtutes funt. Bern. *Serm. 2. in cap. jejunii. pag.* 111. *col.1.K.*

best

beſt *clad* that have their hearts *clothed* with vertue. And therefore
put on meekneſs. Not on your
tongues only, in ſweet and ſugred
words : but on your *hearts* in a quiet
and meek *ſpirit* which before God is
a thing much ſet by. Yea, in the
whole carriage and converſation of
your *lives.*

You muſt ever *put it on,* and ne·
ver *put it off,* until the ſoul *put off* the
body ; you muſt ſit in it, lie down
in it, walk in it, and work in it.

It is a *garment* for all *times,* and
for all *places.*

For all *times,* in the *time* of *wars*
famine, ſickneſs, in the day of trouble and hour of temptation, whe
ſtorms and tempeſts break in upo
us, it is as a *ſafe ſhelter.*

In the *time* of peace, health, plen
ty, in good days which no misfortun
clouds, in Halcion daies when th
Sun of proſperity ſhines upon us;

is as a *pleasant shadow.*

For all *places* ! at *home* within dores in the family, it is as a precious *ointment* to perfume the *house.*

Abroad amongst neighbors, it is as an excellent vertue to season your *conversation* : At the *Market* about your busines : In the *fields*, amidst your Cattel : In the *City* at your vocation : In the *Assembly* at your devotion : on the *Tribunal*, and in the *Pulpit*, *meeknes* agreeth with all *places.* Wherefore it is the wholfome advice of a wise Father to his son. My son go on in thy busines with meeknes, so shalt thou be beloved of him that is approved.

Now *meeknes* as apparel serves for divers uses.

1 In *Indumentum* : for clothing.
2 In *Munimentum* : for defence.
3 In *Ornamentum* : for comlines.

4 In

4 In Momentum : for distinction.

Gen. 3. 7.
Gen. 3. 21.
*Dicitur ve-
stis a ve-
lando, quod
corpus ve-
lat aut
tegat Var.*

First, *Apparel* is for *cloathing* to hide our *nakednes*: and to be a comely *cover* for our more uncomely parts. So *meeknes* serves as a *covering* to *hide and conceal* the brutish rage of our heady *pasions*: and the filthines of our disorder'd *affections*: which should they be seen in their own form, would appear so *monstruous and mishapen* that they would become odious both to God and Man.

For all *affections* and *pasions* they are, as man is, conceiv'd in sin: and sin which hath blemish'd our *understanding* and defaced our purest *mind*, hath made much more deformed and ugly, *affections* and *pasions* which arise from the bruitish part of the soul.

Of these some are more *gentle*; relenting and *tractable* and *easily* drawn to the obedience of *reason*, others more

more *furious sudden and unruly, hard to be tamed and reduced :* such is *Anger,* which leaves a man *naked* , and layes him open to *shame,* and drives the soul from her seat of *judgement,* raises such *commotions and perturbations,* that like a troubled *sea* stirred with a violent *tempest,* the very foundation is shaken, the bottome is discovered, and the Channel appears.

Vide A· it in@Æthic. Intelligentiæ lucem tra subtrahit commentem permovendo confundit. Greg. Moral. lib. 5. Assiliunt fluctus imoque à gurgite

p ntus vertitur, Ovid. 3. Fast. *Quippe sonant clamore viri stridore rudentes undarum incursu gravis unda, tonitrubus æther fluctibus erig tur, cælumque æquare videtur pontus,—— & nunc sublimis veluti de vertice montis, despicere in valles; imaque Acheronta videtur: nam ubi dem ssam curvam circumficit æquor suspicer. inferno summum de gurgite cælum,* Stat.

The passion of *Anger* it deals by men as the *Iews* did by the *Egyptians,* spoyls them of their *jewels and rayment* of *Reason* and *Iudgment*; or as *Aaron* did by the *Israelites ,* makes them *naked* to their *shame :* thus *Anger* makes a man *naked and uncovered,*

Exod. 3.22

Exod. 32. 25. Gen· 9.21

H

Minus ſui compos eſt ira quam ebrietas. Eraſ. So the Fathers term it. *Hier. ad Celantiam. Dum iraſcitur inſanire credatur. Hier. ad Demetri. Ira furor brevis eſt. Horat. Ep. l.1.Ep.2. Greg.* cals anger *mens furore ebria.* Greg. *ſuper Ez. Μαινόμε-*

ed, like *Noah* in his Tent; for *Anger* is the *drunkenneß of the ſoul*, it is a *ſhort madneß* by which a man is carried away from himſelf with heat and choler unto ſuch unhanſome and unmanly *behaviour*, that he becomes a ruful *ſpectacle*, beſides the deformity that lurks within; hence it is that in the whole nature of things there is not a more prodigious *Monſter* than an *angry man*. But *Reaſon* and *Religion* like the two ſonnes of *Noah*, *Sem* and *Iaphet*, take that *garment* of *Meekneß* to cover him. By the help of *Reaſon* a man may do much; but by the help of *Grace* and *Religion* a man may do much more in order to the quieting and ſetling the

θα πάντες ὁπόταν ὀργισώμεθα. Menander *Iratum ab inſano tantum tempore diſtare puta.* Ca. m.

Ora tument ira, nigreſcunt ſanguine venæ, lumina Gorgoneo ſævius angue micant. Ovid. lib. 3 d. art. Am.

Qualia poetæ infernalia monſtra finxere ſuccincta ſerpentibus & igne & flatu, &c. perlege cap. 35. Senecæ in lib. 2. de ira, ubi elegantiſſima deſcriptio irati. Gen. 9 23.

affections

affections, which when they are unruly muſt not be *ruin'd,* but *rectified.*

Affections and *paſſions* were in the firſt Adam in the time of his *innocency* without preturbation ; and in the ſecond *Adam* in the time of his *incarnation* without ſin : yea God himſelf is ſaid to be (ἀνθρωποπαθῶς) Angry, and to hate not really but Analogically; for in him is no motion or commotion, neither paſſion or perturbation, he hath ſaid it of himſelf, and well he might without tax of pride or injuſtice *ego Deus & non mutor.*

Christ alſo took upon him, our *paſſions* with our *nature,* he was not Ἀπαθὴς no ſtupid ſtoick but (as Saint James ſaid of *Elias*) he was of like *paſſions* and *affections* with us: and the author to the *Hebrews* tells us he

Kemnitius Harm. Evang. c. 49. p. 640 col. 2.
Luke 13. 27.
Pſal. 5. 5. Deut 9. 28 Exod. 32. 10, 11 Num. 11. 1 & 16. 22.

James 5. 17.

Heb. 2. 17 Heb. 4. 15. Heb. 5. 3.

In humana Chriſti natura duo conſideranda ſunt, eſſentia carnis & affectus, quare Apoſtolus docet non carnem modo hominis ipſum induiſſe ſed affectus quoque omnes qui ſunt hominum proprii. Calv. Expoſ. in Heb. cap. 3. ver. 17.

had

had a fellow-feeling of our *infir-mities.*

Mat. 23.
23.
Mark. 3. 5. There was an *Antipathy* between our ſins and him; he did loath them, and was ſorry for them, and angry at them.

But there was a *Sympathy* between his *pasſions* and ours which in him were *puniſhments, not ſins* : in us they are both, for the tranſgreſſion of *A-dam* ſo diſorder'd the whole frame of *nature,* that to this day there is a *Schiſm* in the ſoul, the *inferiour facul-* Gal 5. 17. *ties* rebelling againſt the *ſuperiour,* and *pasſion* fighting againſt *Reaſon:* for naturally in man ſince the fall Rom. 8. 7. there is (ἡ ἀσύνετ☉ καρδία) a *fooliſh wilfull heart* that will not be adviſ'd, ſo over-maſtred with *pasſion* that it will not yeeld to enlightned *Rea-ſon.*

How ſhall this *difference* be com-poſed, and this *rebellion* of the *pasſions* quieted, the *Stoicks* preſcribe a *Reme-* *dy dy* worſe than the *diſeaſe,* (to deſtroy them) but Saint *Hierom* likes not this way (which were, ſaith he, *hominem de homine tollere,* to unman a Man, ſeeing the *paſſions* are inſeparably united to our human *nature,* which when it is out of order muſt be rectified not deſtroy'd.

As therefore in a popular *Tumult* and *inſurrection,* ſome grave wiſe man interpoſes himſelf, who with the reverence of his perſon, ſweetneſs of language, and prudent and diſcreet behaviour doth overawe and perſwade them. So *Jeſus Chriſt* the great *Mediator* of peace between *God* and *Man,* he ſo moderates the *paſſions* that he makes *peace* in man, he ſubdues the *will* of the *fleſh* to the Law of the *ſpirit,* makes paſſion yield to *reaſon,* cuts the nailes, and hair of the *bondwoman,* reconciles *Sarah* and *Hagar,* and makes them quietly inhabite under one Roof. Thus *Chriſt*

H 3 *Jeſus*

Tum pietate gravem meritis ſi forte virum quem conſpexere ſilent arrectiſq; auribus aſtant: ille regit dictis animos & pectora mulcet. Virg. Æneid. 1.
Turbatum cælum tempeſtateſque ſerenat. Idem. ibid.
Rom. 7. 25.
Deut. 21. 12.
Gal. 3. 28.

Jesus hath shew'd us a way to cure
our *passions* not to kill them ; to qualifie their *heat*, to rectifie their *disor-*
der, to heal their *distemper*, gently to
lead them, and sweetly to *incline*
them to their proper *objects* : not to
take them away, *ne sint*, that they be
not at all : for that cannot be without
the destruction of the whole man ,
so long as the soul dwels in the body,
there will be *passions* in the soul
(whatsoever the *stoicks* say to the
contrary:but so to compose them, *ne*
obsint, that they hurt not.

A *Christian* must deal with his
passions as the *Apothecary* doth with
poysons, who to make his *confections*
more palatesome, and yet more o-
perative, qualifies the malignity of
simples by preparing them ; making p yson not only medicinable,
but delightfull, and so both cures and
pleases.

The *passions* thus handled by the
                                    discreet

Humphrey
Sydam in
his Sermon
called the
Waters of
Marah and
Meribah n
Rom. 12. 1.

difcreet *Chriftian*, they are wholly conceal'd, and nothing of them appears but fo feemly clad in the habit of *Meeknefs* that they loofe their *venome* and *malignity*, and are a help no hinderance to the foul in the *operations* of it.

Meeknefs is a *Garment* that well futes a *Chriftian* man, but in fome *Cafes*, upon fome *occafions* at fome *times*, with fome *perfons* (Anger) is very feafonable and feemly, we may be *angry*, but we muft not *fin*: for there is an *anger* without *fin* ; and if you will be *angry* and *fin* not, be *angry* at *fin*. When you fee Gods *Name* difhonoured, his *fervice* neglected, his *day* prophaned, his good *fpirit* defpited, here is a fair occafion for the exercife of *anger*: the leaft difgrace in our own *perfons* ; or damage in our own *eftates* toucheth us near, and for thefe men will ftorm, and fret and vex themfelves, and no gentle per-

Eph. 4 26.

fwafions

*Discamus
exemplo
Christi no-
stras inju-
rias mag-
nanimiter
sustinere,
Dei autem
injurias,
nec usque
ad auditum
sufferre.&c
Chrysost.
super illa l.
Mat. 5. qui
dixerit,
&c.
In propriis
injuriis pa-
tientem es-
se laudabi-
le est, inju-
rias autem
Dei dissi-
mulare im-
pium est.
Chrysost.
in Joh 8.
tom 54.
Vide Basil.
mag. orat
de ira.
Hoc enim
non estemen*

svasions can move them to *meekneß;*
and shall we be so tender and sensible
of that which *concerns our selves,* and
so careless and sensleffe of that which
concerns God, ill do we deserve to have
so good, and so gracious a God, who
giveth us all things that pertain to
life and godlines, when we are so
cold in his cause, whereas indeed there
can be no surer sign of an upright
heart, then to be more sensible of the
indignities offer'd to God then of our
own dangers; for certainly no inge-
nious disposition can be so tender of
his own *disgrace,* as the true Christian is of the *dishonour* of God.

If our *affections* were right and
kindly that which *displeases* God
should also *displease us,* and all excess
in our *affections* should run this way,
we may be *passionate* for God, and a-
gainst sin, but we must beware we
pretend not *indignation* against sinne
when we intend *satisfaction* of a self
humour.

humour. It is good to be *zealous* in a good thing alwaies, but all *zeal* is not good:we muſt not take that for a ſpiritual *temper* which is but a natural diſtemper. For ſome are *zealous* out of envy (this was *Cains zeal* :) ſome out of *choler* , (this was *Jonas zeal* :) ſome out of *Hypocriſie*, (this was Je-*hues zeal* :) Some out of *ignorance*, (this was the *Jewes zeal* :) but ſome for the *glory of God*,(this is a *true Chriſtian godly zeal* :) true *zeal* cannot *ſtand* by, and be ſilent when it ſees God *diſhonoured*; and the ſoul *endangered*. *Moſes* was the *meekeſt* man alive,yet will not Moſes ſit ſtill,and ſay nothing, when he ſees the *Congregation* corrupted ; the *peace* of Iſrael diſturbed,the *magiſtracie* and the *prieſthood* queſtioned, if men will be *factious,ſacrilegious and unruly*, it is then time for *Moſes* to ſhew himſelf to be *Moſes*, (Gods *miniſter* and their *magiſtrate*). And a greater *prophet* then *Moſes*

dare me,ſed
vitio tuo
ſatisfacere.
Hieron *ad
Ruſticum
Monachum*
Gal.4. 18.
*Quidam
non ferunt
charitatis
Spiritu,ſed
ſtudio va-
ritatis.*Ber.
Serm. *de
Nativ.* Jo.
Bapt. pag.
216. col.2.
L.
Jude 11.
1 John 3.
12.
Jonas 4.1.
2Kings 10
16.
Rom.10.2.
Acts 22.3.
John 2.17.
Titus 2.14
Rev.3. 19.
Num.12.3.
Num. 16.

Mo*ses* yet no le*s* *meek* (Je*sus* Chri*st* the righteous) who had not a *word* to

Mat.27.14

say for *himselfe* : yet in his *fathers* cau*se* when he sees the *Temple*, the hou*se* of God, the *house* of prayer, made a *house* of *merchandize*, a *den* of theeves, hath a *scourge* to la*sh* the pro-

Jo.2.15,16
Jo.1.29,36

phaners of the Sanćtuary, the *Lamb* of God will sometimes *s*hew him*self*

*Virtus si-
quidem di-
scretionis
absq; cha-
ritatis fa-
vore jacet,
& fervor
vehemens
absq; dis-
cretionis
temperamen-
to praecipi-
tat, idque
laudabilis
cuinextrum
deest qua-
tenus &
fervor dis-*

to be the *Lyon* of J*udah*, thus with Chri*st* and Mo*ses* (when a good *cause* wants it, and a lawfull *call* warrants it,) we may put on a ju*st* *disdain*, a zealous *anger* again*st* the enemies of *Religion* and *peace*, endeavoring by all good means to informe the *judgments* of such as are contrary minded ; and to reform the *practice* of such as are ill-manner'd, but in thus doing we mu*st* joyn *discretion* with *zeal* : le*ft*

cretionem erigat, & discretio fervorem regat. Bern. *super Cant.* Ser. 23. p. 628. *est ergo discretia non tam virtus quam moderatrix & auriga virtutum ordinatrixq; affectuum, & morum doctrix.* Bern. *super Cant.* Ser. 49. pag. 713. D.

like

like a blind *Archer* (who thinking to
have flain a beaft, kil'd a man) inftead
of mending a *friend* we make not a
foē wounding him in his name : when
we fhould win him to God.

And herein is to be obferv'd both
a *due time,* and a *right order.*

1. A *due time* for every thing is
beautifull in its *feafon* ; and what is
out of *feafon* is out of *reafon,* there is
a *time* for all things, *publick offences*
muft be openly reprov'd, but he that
offends in *private* muft be privately
admonifhed.   If thy brother offend
tell him his fault, between thee and
him alone, left thou difgrace his perfon when thou wouldft heal his cor-

*Eme., eme
a Domino
moderatam
correptio-
nem, quia
omnino
quoddam
bonum &
datum op-
timum eft,
& quod ha-
beant pau-
ci.* Bern.
Serm. 2. *de
Refur. Do-
mini.
Sunt quæ-
dam mollif-
fima fan-*

di *tempora, fingula quæque locum tentant forlita decenter.* Horat. *de arte* Poët.

*Temporibus medicina valet data tempore profunt, & data non
apto tempore vina nocent.* Johannes Herodem *quia publice pec-
cabat publice arguebat.* Bonavent. *in cap.* 3. Luc.

*Sæpe gravius vidi offendere animos auditorum, eos, qui ali-
ena flagitia aperte dixerunt quam eos qui commiferunt.* Cicer.
refp. ad Saluft.

Ecclef. 3. 11. Prev. 25. 11,12. Ifa. 50. 4. Ecclef. 3. 1. 1 Tim. 5. 20.
Mark 7. 33. Matth. 18. 15. 2 Sam. 1. 20.   ruption

1 Sam. 25.
22, 23.
1 Sam. 25.
36, 37.
Mat. 23.
24.
Mat. 7. 3, 4,
5.
ruption, moroever as thou must refrain *reprehension* in the *heat* of thy *passion*, so also in the *heighth* of his *sin*.

Abigal is commended for her *discretion* that she watched her opportunity, and dealt with *Nabal*, not in his *drunkennesse*, but when he was *sober*: then she told him freely both of his *sin*, and of his *danger*.

2. A *due order* must be observ'd, and as every sin is greater, so must vve be more incens'd against it. We must not svvallovv a *Camel* and stumble at a *straw*; be troubled at a *moat* and pass by a *beam*; vve must not be more moved at some *small offence* vvherein our selves are concern'd; then at a *far greater* that concernes us nothing; to be touch'd vvith an *injury* done agaiust our selves and pass by open *blasphemy* spoken against God; vvere not this to prostitute *religion* to our ovvn *reason*, yea to our ovvn *passion*, and to

*Pectora
rantis of-
fessa malis
non sunt
ictu ferien-
da levi.
Senec. in
Herc. fu-
rente.*

to fet up our *own* intereft, above Gods.

And if in reproving a man would obferve a *due order*, let him begin fiift with himfelf; let him firft *amend* in himfelf what he would *reform* in another. Let him fpend his *fpleen* upon his own *faults*, confume his *anger* and take *revenge* of his own *fins*, and he will learn to deal more mildly with his *offending Brother*; infult not over his imperfections, but lend him an helping hand, and if he err and go aftray, reclaim him in *love*, and with *modefty* reduce him into the right way. If in fome thing he be *deficient*, in fome other things he may be a good *proficient*: be not too *fevere* againft him for the good he *wanteth*, but *love* and *honor* him for the good he *hath*.

Luk.4.23.

Gal.6.1.

Carere debet omni vitio qui in alterum paratus eft dicere. Cicer. refp. in Saluft.

Cum imperio quippe docetur, quod prius agitur quam dicatur; nam doctrinæ fiduciam fubtrahit, quando confcientia linguam præpedit. Greg. Moral. lib. 2. cap. 7.

Reprehenfions

* Iam. 1. 20
*Sunt vitia
animi (sicut
vitia cor-
poris lenī-
ter tra-
ctandi.*
Seneca.
   *Si vis
me corrigi
delinquen-
tem: aptè
increpa,
tantum ne
occultè
mordeas:
qhid enim
mihi pro-
dest, si a-
liis mala
mea refe-
ras sīme ne-
sciente,pec-
catis meis
ima detre-
ctationibus*

Reprehensions are not to be given with *rashnesse* but with good advice; the mind of man is of a weak and tende: constitution, and must not be *chaf'd*, when it should be *suppl'd*. He that would *reclaim* his friend, and bring him to a true and perfect *understanding* of himself, must do it by strength of *reason*; not by heat of *passion*: least he seem rather to please his own *humour* then correct anothers. Eagerness and harshness of *reproof* doth rather *exasperate* then *reduce*; virulency and bitterness doth neither *please* nor *profit*: *reproofes* must be sweetned with *gentle words*, and pleasing *carriage*, least they be thought to proceed rather from *spight and spleen* then any good meaning or *desire* to *work* a man to goodness. (*The wrath of man worketh not the righteousnesse of God.*)

tuis album vulneres & certatim omnibus narres? sic singulis loquaris quasi nulli dixeris? Hieron: *ad Rust. Monachum.*

When

When we would *amend* in any what is *amiss*, it muſt not be done by railing and reviling (raging like a Bear robbed of her whelps) but with tenderneſs and diſcretion, a difference muſt be put between the *ſinner* and his *ſin*, and he muſt ſo be dealt with that his ſin may be *killed*, and he *cured*. Let the righteous ſmite me friendly: but he is no *friend*, and will hardly paſs for a *righteous man* that (with bitter invectives) will *blaſt* my *name*, when with wholſome *inſtructions* he ſhould amend my *life*.

Pro.17.12.

Pſ.141.5.

Aſperitas odium ſævaque bella movet.
Ovid.2. de Arte.

Crimina non homines noſtra Thalia premat. Curando fieri quædam peiora videmus vulnera quæ melius non tetigiſſe fuit. Ovid.

Thus is *anger* to be clothed with *meekneſſe*. But *anger* as it is a heady *paſſion*, and is hardly moderated, ſo is it many times *miſplac'd*, and ſets against *vertue* and *goodneſſe*. Is thine eye evil

Mat.20.15.

evil becaufe I am good ? (faith Chrift) and am I become your enemy becaufe I tell you the truth ? faith Saint *Paul*; *Cain* was of the Devil and flew his Brother; and wherefore flew he him ? becaufe his own works were evil and his Brothers good.

Gal. 4. C.

1 Jo. 3. 12.

Sore eyes cannot endure to look upon a *bright and fhining object*: the fair whitenefs of *innocency*, the luftre and brightnefs that is in *vertue* is an *eye-fore* to malicious men, who fearch for privy *flanders* : and digg the filth out of lewd *tongues*, to caft upon the *innocent*, and think they have made a rich game of their *fpight*, when they have made themfelves moft *vile* and wicked, to make him feem fo.

Anger is never more *hot* and *outragious* then when it fets upon *innocence, truth* and *righteoufneffe*, when *evil* men are incenfed againft the *good*, they

Vide Ter.
Apol. ad-
verfus gen-
tes. cap. 2.
pag. 26.

they know not when to take up, and can never *rest* but in his *ruine*. See it in the *Jews* who so hotly pursue *Christ*, that nothing will satisfie them, till he be *crucified*; if any ask, what *evil* hath he done? we know their hatred is, because he did none *evil*.

The same spirit of *fury* that inflam'd the Jews against *Christ*, set the world on *fire* against *Christians*, which nothing could quench but the

T meritas quædam hominum est quod odio prosequentur meliores, amant pejores. Basil. To. 2 Ep. 87.
Luk. 23 1.
Mat. 27. 23
Lege Justin. *Martyr. in Dial. cum Tryphone*

Judæo pag. 323. *Christianos ad leones tantos ad unum,* Tert. *Apol. adversus gentes cap.* 40. *pag.* 70.

Τȣτο δὲ ἐςιν ὁ λέγω, μὴ καὶ ὑμᾶις πεπιςεύκατε περὶ ἡμῶν, ὁτι δὲ ἐθίοιψ ἀνθρώποις κ̀ μ̄τ τλω ειλαπίνη ἀποςϛεννύντες τοῖς λύχνοις, ἀθϵσμοις μίξϵσιν ἐσκυλιόμϵθά, &c.

Πλεὶ δὲ ὧν οἱ πολλοὶ λέγȣσιν ρ̀οϵπιϛΐϛαι ἄξιον; πό'ρρο γὸ κεχώρηκε τ̄ ἀνθρωπίνης φύσεως. Justin. *Martyr. Dialogum cum Trypho.* Judæo. *pag.* 227. Justin. *Martyr. Apol.* 1. *pro christianis pag.* 43. *ibid pag.* 56, 57.

Ἐ'φ' ἡμῶν δὲ τὸ ὄρμα ὡς ἔλεγχον λαμβά́νϵτϵ, &c. Just Mart. *Apol.* 2. *pro Christianis. pag.* 55.

Bonus vir Caius Seius, sed malus tantum quod Christianus. Tert. *Apol. adversus gentes. cap.* 3. *pag.* 27.

Haud poterit autem ullo sermone explicari quæ supplicia quosque cruciatus sustinuerunt Martyres. Lege & quæ sequuntur in Euseb. *Eccl. hist. lib* 8. *cap.* 9.

I   blood

Exitiabilis superstitio. Corn. Tacit Annal. lib. 15.

Afflicti suppliciis Christiani, genus hominum superstitionis novæ ac maleficæ. Suet. Traug. in Nero. Cæsaium.

blood of those *Innocents,* it was their *crime* they were *Christians* , and the world *rag'd* against them for no other *reason* but their *religion,* their only *fault* was their *faith* in *Christ,* and for this they are hated, persecuted, defamed, tormented, and wit and malice set on work to devise *strange* and *horrid* deaths, and *hell* it self rak'd for bloody *inventions* to take out of the way the blessed *witnesses* of whom the world was not *worthy*; but

6. *cap.* 16.

Καὶ τὴν αἰτίαν τῆς ἔχθρας εἰπεῖν οἱ μισοῦντες ὐκ ἔχεσιν. Justin Mart. Ep 90. Diog. Μίξεις ἐπ δὲ ἔστρας καὶ λογοποιοῦσιν ἀθέους, Athenagoras lege pro Christianis. pag. 34.

Nero *Quæstissimus pænis affecit , quos per flagitia invisos , vulgus Christianos appellabat.Corn. Tac.annal.lib. 15.*

Ὥπερ ἐστιν ἐν τῷ σώματι ψυχή τῦτ᾽ ἐστιν ἐν κόσμῳ Χριστανος. Just. Mart. Ep. ad Diogn. pag. 497.

Socrat. *Eccl. hist. lib.* 4. *cap.* 24, & 25.

Cæterum, insignis vero & Catholicæ Ecclesiæ splendor, iisdem virtutum vestigiis incedens, & purè vivendi rationis institutio sic mirandum in modum emicuit, ut deformis infamiæ labis, simul cum tempore deleta : ut nemo ex illo tempore turpem aliquam dedecoris maculam, fidei nostræ auderet inferre. Euf. *Eccl. hist. lib.* 4, *cap.* 7.

their

their *meek* suffering did conquer the *cruelty* of their *persecutors,* and over-came the *world,* for at last the splendor of the *Christians lives,* and invincible verity of *their* doctrine, did so prevail and tryumph so victoriously over the *lives* and *tongues* of their e-nemies, that the *blood of Christian Martyrs* became the *seed of Christs Church,* which did spring and grow up with such wonderful encrease, that the world stood amazed to see it self so suddenly become *Christian.*

Lege Le-onem in Serm. 1. de Nat. Pet. & Pauli.San-guis Mar-tyrum se-men Eccle-

si c. Aguft. *in* Pfal. 39. *Nec quicquam tamen proficit exquisi-tior quæque crudelitas vestra ; illecebra est magis, sectæ plures efficimur quoties metimur a vobis ; semen est sanguis Christiano-rum.* Tert. *Apol. adversus Gent. cap.* 50. *pag.* 81. Isa.54.1.

Quis furor, O Cives? quæ tanta dementia? What hellish *fury ?* what *madnesse* in their brains ? with what blind **zeal** was the ignorant ma-licious

Lucan. pharf.

Quid jam attinet nominative reliquorum facere mentionem aut virorum recenſere multitudinem aut varia ſupplicia

licious world tranſported againſt the *truth* and the *profeſſors* of it?

The *Rulers* of the world, who (as God appointed *Moſes*,) ſhould have carried theſe harmleſs *lambs* in their *boſome*, like ravening *wolves* do waſt and devour the *flocks* of *Chriſt.*

ſuſpiciendorum Martyrum deſcribere qui partim ſecuribus cæſi ſunt ſicut contigit in Arabia : *partim fractis crucibus p niti quemadmodum occidit in* Cappadocia. *p utim ex p dibus in ſublime capite demiſſo ſuſpenſi, ignique remiſſiore ſubjecto ardentis materiæ fumo extincti, qualis cruciatus f atribus in* Meſapotamia *illatus eſt ; alicubi etiam naribus, auribus, ac mannibus mutilati, &c.* Euſ. *Eccl. hiſt. l.b.* 8. *cap.* 12.

Iſa. 49. 23.   Iſa. 1. 17.   Numb. 11. 12.

Archilus *dixit* Ju *licem &* Aram *idem eſſe, p riter enim ad utrumque confugiunt qui injuria afficiuntur.* Eraſ. *Apotheg.* The Poet cals the Magiſtrate. ποιμὴν λαῶν Hom. *Iliad.* Πάλιν εἰ μηδὲν Διὰ τε τὴν ϖρεσπρείαν τῇ δρόματος, και Διὰ τὴν πολιτείαν ἐρεισκύμεθα ἀδικοῦντες, ὑμέτερον ἀγωνιᾶσαι ὅτι, μὴ ἀδίκως κολάζοντες τοῖς μὴ ἐλεγχομένοις, τῇ δίκη κόλασιν ὀφλήσητε. Juſtin. *Martyr. pro* Chri. *Apol.* 2. *pag.* 54.

Δημίων δ' ἔπι τὸ τοιοῦτον ἔργον ἀλλ' ἐκ ἀρχόντων ἀγαθῶν. Juſt. *Mart. pro* Chriſtianis. Apo. 2. pag. 59.

What

What an evil aſpect the *malicious world* did caſt upon *religion and righteouſneſs* the *hiſtories* of all *ages* ſufficiently ſhew. A ſhadow whereof we have in *Athens,* where by the law of *Oſtraciſm* there was no man of ſpecial eminency permitted to live. It ſo fell out that *Ariſtides* the juſt came under the cenſure of this *law,* who being requeſted by a *certain man* that could not write,(who was to give his voice for the *baniſhment* of *Ariſtides*) to write his name on a *tile* or *ſhell* as the manner was, he queſtioned *the man,* whether *Ariſtides* at any time had done him wrong? he anſwered, no! neither do I know him. But it grieves me (*ſaies the*

Dum teſtulis no mina inſcribunt dicitur illiteratus quidam & plane rudis Ariſtidi uni de plebe teſtulam tradidiſſe petiiſſeque ut inſcriberet Ariſtidem: admirante eo & rogante, num quid Ariſtides in eum admiſiſſet? Nihil inquit neque eſt mihi notus verum ſtomachor quod paſſim juſtum dici audiam: quo audito nihil Ariſtidem ferunt reſpondiſſe, ſed inſcripſiſſe teſtulæ nomen ſuum atque ei illam reddidiſſe. Plutarch. *de vita* Ariſtidis.

man) to hear every one fay *Ariſti-des is a juſt man*. Now here is a plain caſe (*juſtus quia juſtus*) the righ-teous perſecuted for righteouſneſs ſake.

Mat. 5. 10.

But it is no matter of wonder that this *malignant humour* hath ſo much prevail'd amongſt the *Jews* and *Pa-gans*, for we find the *Church* of God when it was ſhut up in one *family* was not free from it , amongſt *Brethren* of the ſame *Father*, and of the ſame *faith* , yet this inveterate *paſsion* breakes all bonds of *relation*, and in-nocent *Joſeph* is hated by his *Fathers* ſons (for his *coat*) for his *coat* ! the *pledg* of their Fathers love : the *En-ſign* of their Brothers honor : in both which reſpects, it ſhould have been unto them *ſacred* and *inviolable* ; and if there had been in them any (the leaſt) *fear* of God, *reverence* to their Father, or *affection* to their Brother, they would not have dar'd to have touched

Gen. 37. 20. Gen. 37. 23.

touched his *coat* with a violent hand, but their inveterate *hatred* having extinguish'd in them all that was of *God*, or good *nature*, and blinded with *pafsion*, they ftrip him of his *coat*, and had rid him of his *life* too, had not a fpecial *providence* reftrained them.   And he that permitted their *malice* ordered it another way, and yet an innocent perfon muft fuffer for his *coats* fake.   Gen.37. 25.

What ufage may *Jofeph* expect from *Ifmaelites* and *Egyptians*, that meets with fuch hard meafure amongft his *Brethren*, an evil *beaft* hath *torn* him (faies the deceived Father) and *rightly*! for what *beaft* fo fierce as inveterate *wrath*. But let them palliate their *malice* with pretences and hide their *cruelties* with a lie, yet the time fhall come; when their eyes which were *blinded* with an ungovern'd *pafsion*, fhall be *opened* with an unexpected *affliction*: and their *fin* and their   Gen.37. 28,35.   Gen.37. 33.   Gen.42. 21.

I 4   Brothers

Brothers *sufferings* shall be brought to their remembrance, and so sadly ! that what drew *tears* from his *eyes*: shall fetch *blood* from their *hearts.*

This was the *lot* of the *righteous* in all *ages*: the *best men* have been persecuted and reproched. *David* a man after Gods own heart complaines, *the mouth of the wicked, and the mouth of the deceitful are opened against me. They have spoken against me with a lying tongue.* *Wrath* is the *hell* that sets on fire a *wicked tongue.* *Passion* blinds *reason*, darkens the understanding that it cannot *discern* the *truth*; puts out the *eyes* of the *soul*: drives a man out of himself: that like a *mad* man, or one that is *drunk*, he saies and does he knows not what.

Gen 42.
22.

Cum itaque Valens *imperator cum* Alexandrinos, *rum* Æ gyptios *persecutionibus adst gi lege præcepisset vastabantur subvertebantur omnia & alii ad Tribunalia trahebantur, alii ve o in carceres conjiciebantur, & alii qt ter torquebantur: varia siquidem supplicia contra quietis amantes exercebantur.* Socrates *Eccl. hist. lib. 4. cap.24.* Psa.109.2. Jam.3.6. *Impedit ira animum ne possit cernere verum.* Cato dist.

The

The Wicked (*sayes David*) *whet their Tongue like a Sword,* they bend their Bow to shoot out their Arrows even bitter Words, they speak Wickedly and loftily, they set their mouth against the heavens. But although *Dogs* bark at the *Moon:* yet still she keeps the *heavens:* and daily runs her conſtant *courſe* in her own *ſphere.* *Goodneſſe* is never the leſs *good,* becauſe it is *maligned,* and *reproached.* *Anger* is a *fire,* let it be rightly placed (on the *hearth* or in the *furnace*)& it is of ſingular *uſe*:but in *ſtraw* or on the *houſe top,* it ſets all in a *combuſtion.* It is a *paſsion* that is headſtrong : *meekneſſe* is the *bridle* to *check* it. And it muſt have more of the *curb* and leſs of the *raine:* to yield to *wrath* is to yield to the *Devil,* to be ſet on fire againſt goodneſs is *deviliſh.*

Chriſtian prudence will adviſedly conſider what is fit for every ſtate and

Pſal.6 4.3.
Pſal.64. 3, 4
Pſal.73.8, 9.

Eph.4.26. 27.

and condition of *men*, and will deal with them with all *meeknesse* : putting a difference, saving some with fear, on others having compassion.

Jude 23.

Some are *unruly*, and must be *sharply admonished* : some are *wilful* and *obstinate* and must be *terrified* : some are *weak* and must be *supported* : others *feeble-minded* & must be *comforted* : and some are *tractable* and must be gently *entreated*, ever *hoping* well of those in whom there is any thing of *grace* or of *God*.

1 Thes. 5. 17.

Semper bene spe-randum de eo in quo cernimus aliquid Dei. Calvin. in Johan.

And if we meet with any that are *froward* we must not reject them, but do as God does ; follow them with *mercy* and new *offers* of *grace*, pitying and praying for them.

We must *bear* one anothers *burdens*, it is sure there is *corruption* in all : every one hath some *fault* or other : some are *hasty*, some are *suspicious*, some are *covetous*, we must *bear* one with another, let every one of

Gal. 6. 2.

Rom. 15. 2.

of us *pleafe* his neighbour for his good to edification, and fpeak evil of no man, be no brawlers, but gentle, fhewing all meeknefs unto all men.

Quicquid in alio reprehenditur id unufquifque in finu fuo inveniet. Sen. lib.

3. *de ira cap. 26. Omnes inconfulti & improvidi fumus omnes incerti, queruli, ambitiofi, quid lenioribus verbis hucus publicum abfeendo? omnes Mali fumus. idem ibid. Tit. 3. 2*

2. In *Monumentum,* a *fecond ufe* of *Apparel* is to *defend* and *protect* the body from *cold, heat,* and *outward harmes;* fo ! *meeknefs* is a fure *defence,* and ferves as a *wall of brafs* to protect from danger, that no ftorms or tempefts of injury, flanders, afflictions can hurt us. It only knows by *yielding* how to *overcome,* and to *triumph* over the *conqueror.* Meeknefs (like *Medufa's head*) ftrangely aftonifhes all that behold it : for when *rage* and *cruelty* meet with an unexpected *meeknejfe* and *humility,* how fuddainly many times is *fury* turn'd

turn'd into *mercy*. The *Lion* dif-
dains to prey upon him, who lies
proftrate before him : and we find by
experience that no force or outward
vio'ence, is of that power as *meek-*
neffe is : for the one *fubdues* the *body*,
but the other *enthrals* the *heart*, and
conquers the moft valiant *mind*. He
that knows not to be *overcome*, and
returns *victorious* from many a *battle*,
yields himfelf a captive to *meekneffe* ;
all his powers fall a *fhaking* , and all
his ftrenghthand courage *fails* him,
when *meekneffe* doth oppofe him.
The *tongue* of the *meek* wifely guided
hath as *fharp an edg* as the *fword* of
the *mighty* and more enemies have
been vanquifhed, and more Coun-
tries fubdued by *courtefie* then *cruelty*.
And experience teacheth us that a
yielding eafineffe hath been preferv'd
when a *refifting ftubbornneffe* hath
been ruin'd.

In a *violent tempeft*, the ftiff and
stubborn

ftubborn *Oakes* are overturn'd, when
the pliable and bending *reedes* and
ofiers have been fafe.

The piercing *lightning* when it
breaks forth, *cleaves affunder* things
hard and which *refift it* : but meeting
with things *foft* and *giving place*; it
doth eafily *penetrate* and *hurts them
not.* For when *violence* meets with
violence, it threatens the ruine of one
or both, when *wrath* encounters with
wrath, the conflict is or *dangerous* or
defperate.

Wherefore our *Saviours* precept
is a good rule (refift not evil.) And
St. Paul teaches the fame leffon,
avenge not your felves, and this is no
new commandment, but found in
the old Teftament, Lev. 8. 19.
*Thou ftalt not feek reveng, neither
fhalt thou keep in mind the injury of thy
people.* (faith *Salomon*) I will do to
him as he hath done to me, I will reward him according as he hath de-
ferved

*Nam ira-
cundia per
iracundi-
am non
compefcitur
fed ampli-
us irrita-
tur.* Chry-
foft.
Mat. 5. 39.
Rom. 12. 19.

Lev. 8. 19.

Pro. 24. 29.

Quanto satius est sanari injuriam, quam ulcisci. Sen. de ira lib. 3. cap 27.

ferved. *Prov.* 24. 29. VVouldſt thou live in *peace* and win thine *enemy*? the way to do this is not to *vex* him, overcome him (if poſsible) with *kindneſſe,* if that will not work: *neglect him : forget him*: and he will the ſooner remember himſelf : the end of *paſsion* is many times the beginning of *repentance.*

Thus muſt we deal (in *meekneſſe*) and that in obedience to the word of God, leaſt we divert the courſe of *Gods juſtice* (which aimed at our enemies) upon our *own heads*; for whilſt men follow their *own luſts,* in ſeeking *revenge* againſt the *mind of God :* the *Judgments of God* do fol-

Nullum tam ar-ctum eſt Jugum quod non minus lædat ducentem quàm repugnantem. Senec. de ira lib. 3. cap. 16.

Conſentiam itaque adverſario meo, cedam denique urgenti aculeo ne bis pungat. Parcetur enim ei qui ſenſerit & dederit locum iræ. Bern. Serm. de verbis Domini, *omnis qui ſe exaltat bumiliabitur.* In fine pag. 392. col. 1. G.

low

3

low them, which many times take
place, in the *ruine of their own fami-
lies*; and they in wraftling with the
hatred and wickednefs of other men,
to their own deftruction, waft themfelves, their friends, their goods,
deprive themfelves of all reft, and
many times *fall into mifchief*,whereas
the *meek* and *patient* (befides the
hope of future bleffednefs in heaven)
find a recompence here on earth, to
live in peace and quietnefs: their
names continue: their *houfes* ftand:
their *pofterity* encreafe: they keep
their *leaf* and *greeneffe*: and enjoy
the fruit of the *promifes* of this *life*,
and *that which is to come.*

Mat.5.5.

He therefore that would live in
fafety, muft ftudy to be *quiet* and live
in *peace*; for he that lives not in
Charity on earth, fhall never live in
Glory in heaven; he therefore that
forgives an enemy, *furthers* himfelf;
for in fo doing he heaps coals upon
his

his head, by making his Reckoning
the more, and his own the less.

Now he that would live in quiet,
must be careful of two things.

1. *To decline all occasions of the quar-*
rel.

2. *To inure himself to meekness.*

First, he must decline all occasions of Quarrel; for truly it is a great
fault in some (who otherwise may
be both *wise* and *good*) to be too
tender and too *inquisitive.*

Too *tender*, by laying to heart
what men say of them.

Too *inquisitive*, what such an one
or such an one says.

Whereas in *prudence* they should
not seem to *know*, or not seem to
mind what is said, at least not to be
too *inquisitive* after the Author ; for
by this means, a man may *mend* himself

felf and not *malice* the perfon.

We know what the *Jews* faid of *John* and of *Iefus* : but *wifdom* is ju-ftified of her *Children.*

Moreover, too much *Iealoufie* Mat.11.19. may apprehend a *wrong* when it is none; be fure of proofs that carry in them weight and conviction, o-therwife whilft men feek to *revenge* an injury, they may *begin* one.

Rafhnefs, ignorance, or a mif-un-derftanding may pafs for an *excufe* with a good man, whofe *Conftructi-ons* are ever with *charity and fa-vour.*

Secondly, he that would live in quiet, muft inure himfelf to *Meek-nefs*; for *cuftom* will make a thing *eafie* and *familiar.*

Milo by bearing a *Calf* daily, was

Magis urgent fæ-va inex-
pertos, *grave eft teneræ cervici jugum.* Senec. *lib. cur bo-nis viris mala fiant. cap. 4.*

Nihil miferum eft quod in naturam confuetudo perduxit. Se-neca. *ibid.*

K   ab!e

able to bear it, when it was an *Ox*: how eaſie will he bear the *injuries* of malicious men, that hath attain'd the habit of *Meekneſs*; it is nothing to ſuch an one to be *reviled* or *ſlandered*, who can paſs by evil language with neglect and contempt.

Neglect will ſooner kill an *injury* than *Revenge*; all the *harm* a common *ſlanderer* can do with his *foul mouth*, is but to *ſhame himſelf*; and to ſeem to be touched with an *injury*, is an *advantage* which an enemy *looks* for.

Contempt is the beſt *Remedy* in a cauſe-leſs *wrong*; for to *contemn* an enemy that is full of *malice*, but wants *might*, is better than either to *fear him*, or *anſwer him*: in ſuch a caſe, *contempt* of an injury and *Courteſie* to him that *offers* it, puts both out of *Countenance*. Thus *Meekneß* begets *peace* and *quietneſs*, by ſetting a man in a way to pacifie

an

Ut quiſqu; contemptiſſimus, & ut maxime ludibrio eſt, ita ſolutiſſimæ linguæ eſt. Senec. lib. in ſap. non cadere injuriam. cap. 11.

an enemy by *silence* and *softnes*.

1. By *silence* : *Anger* is a short *frenzie* : what *profit* is it, nay what *folly* were it, to exchange words with one that is *frantick*. Return not then reviling with reviling ; but if an enemy set *fiercely* upon us, and open his mouth *wide* against us, give way, let him vent his *spleen*, and the storm will quickly *ceafe* : let him alone, and he will the sooner come to himself : the way to break an enemies spight, is not to meet him in his fury, to give rebuke for rebuke, but rather give place to wrath : *Anger is the sicknes of the mind* : he that would *cure* the sick, must not administer *physick* in the fit. So if thy neighbour be *angry*, *forbear* him ; give *place* for the present, *deal* not with him in the fit, but *set upon* him when he is more *calm and capable of Counsel*.

Outragious pasions are violent and

Quis enim phrenetico medicus ira- citur idem ibid.

against

againſt nature (*as a ſtone forced up-*
ward) ſtrong at the beginning, and
the further it paſſeth, the more it
weakneth, until at laſt it return to
the natural courſe again : therefore *a*
little ſpace muſt be given for the *paſ-*
ſionate to draw back, for the *patient*
to put forward. *Paſſion* prevails on
the ſudden, but R *eaſon* gathers force

Primi ejus
ictus acres
ſunt, ſicut
ſerpentium
veneni a
cubili re-
pentium
nocent : in-
noxii den-
tes ſunt,
cum illos
frequens
morſus
exhauſit Se-
nec lib. de
ira 1. cap.
16.
Pro. 15. 1.
1Cor. 4. 12.

by leaſure. *Serpents* when they
firſt creep out of their *dens,* are full
of *poyſon* , their *ſting* is mortal, it
were *madneſſe* to abide their *bites* ;
but after they have ſpent their *venom*
with frequent *bitings,* you may
handle them without *harm.*

Secondly, By *ſoftneſs* is anger pa-
cified ; a ſoft anſwer turneth away
wrath, which Saint *Paul* and his fel-
low *Apoſtles* knew full well , and
therefore they went a *meek* way to
work with their enemies ; *being re-*
viled (ſay they) *we bleſs : being*
perſecuted, we ſuffer it : being defamed,
we

we intreat : and this Courſe muſt we take, if ever we look for *peace* with God, or *comfort* in our Souls.

And ſurely there is little *ſafety* to him that is *haſty*, raſh, or eaſily angry ; for *Anger* makes many *enemies*, divides *friends*, turns *love* into *paſsion*, *paſsion* into grievous *words*, and ſometimes *words* into *blows* ; and then a *third Adverſary* to both, hath a *fair Advantage* to inſult over them. *Judah* is hot againſt *Iſrael*, *Iſrael* againſt *Judah*, and the *King of Syria* ſmites them both.

And the common enemy of *Mankind*, whilſt we in heat *wound* one another, *wins* upon us all. If men will be *contentious*, let them *contend* as *Ariſtides* and *Themiſtocles*, ſtrive to exceed one another in *vertue*.

We read of the *King of Iſrael*, that he commanded to ſet *bread and water* before the hoaſt of the *King*

of

of Syria when he might have slain them ; and he lost nothing by it, but by his courteous and gentle using them, he did so work upon them, that he prevented *succeeding quarrels*, so that the bands of *Aram* came no more into the land of *Israel*.

He that would live *securely*, must live *peaceably* ; for by *Contention* comes no good : to strive with a *superiour* is *madnes* : with an *equal*, *doubtful* : with an *inferiour*, *sordid* and *base* : with any full of *unquietnes*.

Let every man therefore refrain his *spirit* ; for when men that are hasty and given to quarrel, do meet, it is as when the *flint* and *steel* do clash, the issue is fire, and how great a matter will a little *fire kindle* : and when the *fire* begins to *kindle*, who knows where it may end ; it may begin in a poor *Cottage*, but ends in the ruin of Princes *Palaces*.

Break off the beginnings of *strife* ; for

for *anger* to the mind, is as a *coal* on the *flesh* or *garment*, caſt it off ſpeedily, it doth *little harm*, let it lie, it *frets* deeply.

The beginning of *ſtrife*, is, as when one letteth out water, like a breach in the ſea, therefore the Wiſeman well adviſeth, *leave off contention before it be medled with. How many are there who have ſuffered a *ſword* in their *bowels*, becauſe they would not ſuffer a *lye* in their *throats*; and a *raſh word* hath been ſometime the occaſion of a world of *blood-ſhed.*

It is a proverb, *the haſty man ſeldom wants wo*; for it is with a man given to *wrath*: as it is with a man given to *wine*: who hath wo? who hath ſorrow? who hath wounds without cauſe? *Prov.* 23. 29. for a mans haſty ſpirit *hunts* him into *ſnares*: whereas of *ſuffering comes eaſe*: eaſe and quietneſs is the effect of quiet

K 4　　　　　ſuffering

*Pro.*17.14 Parva verba multoties homicidium perpetaverunt Chriſ.in Mat.5. ſuper illud qui dixerit fratri ſuo fatue quoſdam unius verbi contumelia, non æquo animo lata in exilium projecit: & qui levem injuriam ſilentio ferre noluerint, graviſſimis malis obruti ſunt. Senec. de ira. lib. 2. cap.14. prope fi. nem. Pro.23.29.

Mat. 11.
29.

suffering ; *Learn of me* (saith Chrift) *for I am meek and lowly, and ye fhall find reft for your fouls* ; for if a man obferve it, when he can bear *injuries,* and pafs by *indignities,* and fuffer *reproaches quietly* he fhall find fuch a *tranquillity* in his fpirit, fuch *peace* and *content* in his heart, as if he had gained fome *victory.* But a man may wrong himfelf in being too *gentle* and *patient* ; for put up one *injury,* and you fhall have enough : to pafs by one *injury,* is to draw on another : the *Afs* doth never want a *burden,* becaufe he never refufes to *bear* one: and he that makes himfelf a *fheep,* fhall be fure to be hunted (if not devoured of the Wolf.) *Malice* delights to fet her *foot* upon the neck of *meekneß :* and patience makes prefumption infolent.

*Veterem
ferendo
injuriam
invites no-
vam. Aul.
Gel. noct.
Attic.lib.
18.*

For fome are fo *wild* and *hairbrain'd :* fome fo *knotty* and *crofsgrain'd,* fo *dogged* and *furly* ; that

         they

they are capable only of the Re-
ftraint of fear. *Meeknefs* to fuch had
need to be guided with *wifdom,* left
it prove *cruel* to it felf. It were
madnefs, not *meeknefs* to tender the
throat to an unjuft *ftroke,* or to give
an enemy occafion to *infult.*

It is *difcretion* fo to bear an *injury,*
as not to encourage an enemy : he
that hath wronged one without
controul, threatens many. *Lawful
Remedies* profecuted with modefty
and gentlenefs are warranted before
God and man.

Chriftians , though it is their
praife, they are *meek and patient* : yet
are they not ftocks and ftones, unfen-
fible of *wrongs* and *injuries :* do they
feel the *fmart* , and fhall they not
feek for *eafe ?* no queftion, endeavour to *right* themfelves they may,
revenge themfelves they may not.

And becaufe the good *nature* of
the *meek* lies open to abufe, it will
not

not be amiſs to put in here a *Caveat* or two.

Let him beware of being too *credulous,* or too *timerous.*

The *meek* is apt to be too *Credulous :* not conſidering that the Snake lurks in the graſſe, it is not *wiſdom* to be *ſuſpicious* without cauſe: and it is *weakneſſe* to be too *credulous* upon every cauſe. Believe not every ſpirit, *all is not gold that gliſters : enemies* ſometimes mask under the vizard of *friends :* who have *honey* in their *mouths,* but *poyſon* in their *hearts;* their words ſmoother than butter, but war in their hearts ; like the *Bee* that will *ſting* moſt when ſhe is fulleſt of *honey.* Of ſuch treacherie *David* complains. It was not an open enemy that reproached him, but his own familiar friend whom he truſted: and what ! Thou my ſonne (ſayes *Cæſar*) take heed of ſuch that with *Joab* will *ſalute* you *kindly,* when they

1 Joh.4. 1.

Pſal.55.21.

Pſal. 41.9.

2 Kin.3.27

they hate you *deadly* : *smile* in your face, and *stab* you at the *heart* : and *Judas* like, will offer a *kiße*, when they intend to *kill* : subtle and hollow-hearted, who will undermine you, and do you a *mischief*, and you shall never know who *hurt* you : pestilent and plaguie fellows that meditate deceit : who like dangerous Curres, will *bite* and never *barke* : or like a slaughterman, that will clawe the *Oxe* on the back, that he may the better lay the *beetle* on his head, These are those *white Devils*, who when they speak fair, beleeve them not : for there are seven abominations in their heart: a false friend is like *Solomons harlot*, whose *lips* drop as an *honey-comb*, and her *mouth* is smoother than *oyle*, but her *houſe* is the way to *hell*, going down to the chambers of death, who will hunt for the precious life.   Now how much better are the *laſhes* of a real *friend*, than the *kiſſes*

Mat. 26. 49

Pro. 26. 25

Prov. 5. 3,

Prov. 6. 26,

of

of a *foe*.   Beware ! there are none more quickly ruin'd, than thoſe who are moſt ſecure ;   remember what *Jael* did to *Siſera*, and if thou deſireſt to approve thy ſelf *Meek*, yet do not like a tame *fool*, run thy *neck* into e-very *nooſe* ; our Maſter would have us to learn of *Serpents*, but to beware of *men*.

Judg. 4. 21

Mat. 10. 16
     17

Secondly, ſometimes they are too *timerous*,   take heed of timidity, too much *fear* will put a man beſides his meekneſſe , *fear* of a *danger* ſome-times cauſes a man to fall into the *danger* he *fears*.

Fear not big words, nor a blabbing tongue , which like *ſquibs* , fire, crack, and flame, and vaniſh in an in-ſtant, and leave no remembrance that they have been , but a *ſmoak* and a *ſtink*.

A lewd tongue, and a loud mouth when they begin to move and open, as if they would blaſt and deſtroy :
                                             fear

fear them not, for the moſt part, though their will be *great*, their power is *little*. In malice they are *Giants* and *Dragons*, in might *dwarfes* and *flies*. Like a kind of Serpent, which being full of *poyſon*, yet being *toothleſſe*, hurts none but it ſelf.

And in their reviling they may perhaps do a man more good than they think for; like one, who *ſmiting* another, thinking to *kill* him, broke his *Impoſtume*, and perfectly cur'd him.

But here I take it not to be impertinent to offer in an humble advice about *Meekneſ̃*, to take heed of Miſtakes, *Lenitude* and Remi*ſneſ̃* of ſpirit, may not paſſe for *meekneſſe*: for a man to be ſo devoted to his private ſafety, as to give over himſelf to eaſe and reſt, without reſpect unto others; that cares not (ſo he may be in quiet, live in peace, and ſleep in a whole skin) though others be vexed, trou-

troubled and torn; this is not a temper sutable to thofe Rules of *Christianity* which the *Gospel* layes before us.

Ne præponas conco:-diam veritati, sed generofe perfistas ad mortem ufque. Chryfoft. *in illud* Pauli *ad* Rom. *quantum in vobis pacem cum omnibus habentes.*

Men that care not what becomes of R*eligion*, let the *Church* finke or fwim , fo they may thrive and live free from trouble. In fuch a cafe to part with *truth*, to purchafe *peace* . is a hard *bargain*; and fuch an one as never enrich'd the *Chapman* with *gain*; unleffe they make account that Gods difpleafure, and the ruine of their fouls will be advantage ; a dear rate to lofe Gods protection, and incur condemnation : let no man enflave his *judgment* to orher mens *opinions* ; but take courage for the *truth*, and whatfoever trouble or loffe it may bring, recede not from it. Sin is the *fting* of all troubles; pull out the *fting*, and deride the *malice* of the *Serpent*.

Though it breed *anger*, and beget
haterd,

hatred and *malice* ; yet neverthelesse
I tell you the *truth.*

1 John 16. 7.

We must not be so far in love with our own tender ease, as not to vindicate and free the *truth,* when it is opposed or oppressed, Suppose there may be danger in this ingenuity; the good Christian forecasteth it not, or regardeth it not, for he so fixes his eye upon Gods glory , that he doth not so much as reflect on his own safety, whose thoughts being wholly taken up with *zeale* to the common *good:* leave no roome to think of a private *danger.*

And although *wise* and *good* men are taught highly to value their *lives,* where *to die* is not to *obey:* yet the assurance of Gods call and protection (when a mans actions are warranted by the Word) will take away the fear of death which can never startle him who hath this assurance: that being in Gods way, *whilest he is here,*
God

God will protect him : and *when he goes hence*, God will receive him: and therefore to lose life to preserve the *Truth*, there cannot be a more *comfortable death.* It is the *noblest death* that can be, to *die* accompanied with *vertue.* Gracious and good men, what have they not said? What have they not done? What have they not suffered? to vindicate *truth:* and for the maintenance of .true Religion and vertue. It is a signe of a *poor spirit*, and argues a *degenerate mind* to grow out of love with a *discountenanced truth* , and to cleave to some *foul error* that is in request. Yet in pleading for *truth*, a decorum must be kept; an awful *reverence*, and dutiful *obedience* to *Superiours*, whether in nature or place; for God who highly commends *zeale* for his *Truth*, strictly commands *obedience* to higher *Powers:* a reverential distance must be observ'd that God be not evil spoken of.   *Zeale zeal* muſt be ever accompanied with *diſcretion*, reſpect muſt be had to time, and place, and perſons : and the whole buſineſſe muſt be carried on, with meekneſſe and modeſty; if we cannot have truth, but we muſt contend for it, it is beſt contending with the ſword of the Spirit (which is the Word of God) whetted with prayers and teares. If *God* and *Man* ſtand in competition, the Reſolution is a *rul'd caſe* (we ought to obey God *rather* than man:) *Rather*, in reſpect of the danger that attends the diſobeying of either : for it is a fearful thing to fall into the hands of the living God. Men can deſtroy the body, and after that have no more that they can do. God can caſt both (body and ſoul) into hell fire.

The fear of *loſſe*, or hope of *gain*, muſt not ſo benum the *ſenſes*, or corrupt our *reaſon*, as to admit a *great evil*, for a *litle good*. When we ſee

Acts 5.26.

Heb.10 31

Mar.10.28

L   men

men bold and buſie for *error*, even to
impudence; it is a ſhame to be lazie,
eaſie, and ſo addicted to the enjoy-
ments of outward *peace*, that no care
be had what encroachments are made
on *truth*, the trueſt peace and ſafety
is that, which is grounded on *verity*;
which the world can neither give, nor
take away.

Their ſafety, and their quiet, men
do prefer, and juſtly, yet on theſe,
men ſet too high a *price*, when for
them they can ſwallow down any *error*, change their *profeſſion*, be of any
religion, betray the *truth*, and never
look towards them who loved the
truth above their lives.

Men then are *bruitiſh*, when they
ſeek only to live, whoſe *degenerate
thoughts* are all for the preſent ſupply
of back and belly; ſurely of ſuch,
there can be no ſafety to the ſoul, no
quiet in the conſcience; when as to
avoid the *cenſures of men*, they fall
into

into the heavie *Judgment of God*.

The *Meek man* then muſt have a care he ſuffer not a vice to ſteale upon his good nature; for *Remiſneſſe* by no meanes may paſſe for Meek-neſſe.

And he that is *meeke* indeed had need to be very heedful : his caſe be-ing much like that of *Ezechiel* (to be with briers and thornes, and to dwell among Scorpions) the *meek man* Ber-nard fitly reſembles to the Church in the *Canticles*, which is as the *Lillie* among *thornes*. Now the *Lillie* is a fair and flouriſhing *plant*, ſmooth, gentle, tractable, eaſie to be handled; but the ſons of *Belial* are all of them as *thorns*, becauſe they cannot be ta-ken with hands, but the man that ſhall touch them, muſt be fenced with *iron*, and the *ſtaffe* of a ſpear.

The *meek man* thus beſet (like the *Lillie* growing among *thornes*) with the ſons of *Belial* (enemies to peace)

Ezek. 2. 6.
Bern. in
tractatu de
paſſione Do-
mini. cap.
19. de Ra-
dice Lillii.
pag. 1194.
C.

that

that at every blaſt threaten to wound and teare him, muſt be vigilant for the preſervation of himſelf.

To this purpoſe S. *Paul* ſtudious of the ſafety of the Chriſtians (who liv'd amidſt their enemies that were incens'd againſt them) well adviſeth, Rom. 12. 19. *Dearly beloved, avenge* Rom. 12. *not your ſelves, but ra her give place* 19. *unto wrath,* for by this means *enemies* are either *vanquiſhed,* or *appeaſed;* for the *meek* commending himſelf and his matters unto God, by patience and forbearance maketh God for him, who beholdeth miſchief and ſpight to requite it with his own hand, and therefore ſaith the *Pſalm-* Pſal.10. *iſt, the poor committeth himſelf unto* 14. *God, who is the helper of the father-* *leſſe.* When they curſe, God will Pſal. 109. bleſſe, for he ſhall ſtand at the right 28. 31. hand of the poor, to ſave his ſoul from unrighteous Judges; yea, he will break the power of the ungodly and

and malicious: bring the counsel of the Heathen to nought, and make the devices of the people of none effect. Thus God undertakes for the *meek*, and under his protection they rest secure ; for none can *hurt* whom God will *help*, but God is the *helper* of the *meek*; and therefore put on Meeknefs, in M*unimentum*, as a fure defence.

Pfa.10.15.

Pfa.33.10.

Ibi requi-em inve-nit manfu-etus &

fimp'ex, ubi dolofus opprimitur vel elatus. Bern. *fuper* Cant. *Serm. 62. pag. 752. K.*

Thirdly, In *Ornamentum*, a third ufe of *Apparel*, is to beautifie and adorn the body. So *meekneß* is the goodlieft *ornament* of the foul , and is that which renders a man amiable and lovely in his whole life. For *modefty* in the countenance , *gentle-neß* of carraige , *affability* of fpeech, *calmneß* of fpirit, *quietneß* of mind, are lov'd and commended in all. No *plaiting of hair, wearing of* Gold, or

L 3   *putting*

Meeknesse,

putting on of apparel, is an ornament comparable to that of a *meek* and *quiet* spirit, this hath in it a *power* and *sweetneſſ* strangely attractive, and commands all hearts and eyes in the Judgment of Saint *Peter.* Meeknes is an excellent *grace,* which in the heart is *tenderneſſe,* in the diſpoſition *ſoftneſſe,* in the affections *temper,* in the mind *calmneſſe,* in the carraige *ſweetneſſ.*

1 Pet.3. 3,
4.

Doctor
Featley *n*
Clavi Myſtica, Serm. 3. *in* Matth. 12. 19. *pag.* 35.

The excellence of *Meekneſſe* is rarely ſet forth by *Tertullian* in his book of Patience in theſe words.

It ſtrengthens faith, governs peace, helps love, trains up humility, waits for repentance, ſeals up confeſſion, rules the fleſh, preſerves the ſpirit, bridles the tongue, contains the hand, ſuppreſſes temptations, puts away ſcandals, conſummates

mates Martyrdom, comforts the poor, guides the rich, prolongs not sickness, nor destroyes health: refreshes him that believes, invites him that believes not, commends the servant to his Master, the Master to God: it beautifies the woman, it commends the man: it is lov'd in a child, it is prais'd in a young man, honor'd in an old: in every sex, in every age it is lovely. The effigies of meekness by the same Author is thus set forth.

Fidem munit : pacem gubernat ; dilectionem adjuvat, humilitatem instruit : pœnitentiam expectat, exomologesin adsignat, carnem regit, spiritum servat linguam frænat, manum

continet, tentationes inculcat scandala pellit, Martyria consumma', pauperem consolatur, divitem temperat : infirmum non extendit, valentem non consumit fidelem delectat, gentilem invitat, servum Domino Dominum Deo commendat, fæminam exornat, virum approbat : amatur in puero, laudatur in juvene ; suspicitur in sene, in omni sexu, in omni ætate formosa est.
Age jam si effigiem habitumque ejus comprehendamus.

Her countenance calm and pleasing, her forehead smooth, contracted or drawn together with no wrincles of grief or anger, her brows not

L 4 frowning

Vultus illi tranquillus & placidus, frons pura nulla mœroris aut irœ rugositate contracta; remissa æque in lætum modum supercilia, oculis humilitate, non infœlicitate dejectis. Os taciturnitatis honore signatum, color qualis securis & innoxiis:

frowning or sullen, but tempered to a chearful modesty, with eyes cast down not for any misfortue, but in humility; her mouth sealed with the honor of silence, her color and complexion bewrais her innocency, as one that is secure & fears nothing : she often shakes her head against the Devil, and her smiles are threatnings.

But her Apparel about her breast is white and close to her body, which no wind can blow up, nor any motion shake, for she sits in the throne of that most mild and gentle spirit, which no boistrous storm can shake, nor clouds obscure, for with her it is ever fair weather, she is simple and plain, thus far *Tertullian.*

It greatly matters not what some are pleas'd to speak of Meeknesse,

Motus frequens capitis in Diabolum, & minax risus. Cæterum amictus ei cum pectora candidus, & corpori impressus: ut qui nec inflatur, nec inquietatur. Sedet enim in throno Spiritus ejus mitissimi & mansuetissimi qui non turbine glomeratur, non nubilo livet, sed est tenerœ serenitatis, apertus & simplex, &c. Tert. lib. de Patientia. cap. 15. pag. 203.

that it is for *Fools* and *Cowards*, and a note of a poor and meek mind, that it is childish and effeminate, and no *masculine* or *manlike* vertue. And if this were so, then were Meekness rather a *disparagement* than an *ornament*, But that it is not so, but a vertue well becoming the most wise and valiant is apparent.

First, It is an *ornament* to the *wise*, for if *Meeknesse*, quietness and peaceableness had not well become the *wise*, the wisest mans name should not have been *Salomon* (that is *pacificus* , peaceable ;) and the *wisdom that is from above is pure and peaceable, gentle, easie to be entreated, and full of mercy* saith Saint *James.* and the same *Apostle, James* 3. 13. sets it down as a special note to know a wise man by. *Who is a wise man and endued with knowledg among you? let him shew out of a good conversation his works with meekneß of wisdom.* And

Jam. 3 17.

Jam. 3. 13.

however

however the world may account men *wise* that know how to fish in troubled waters, and by keeping up a *schism* in the *Church*, or maintaining a *faction* in the *State*, do make a party; & weaken a common Force by dividing it; or that in private affaires knowes how to over-reach or over-bear their neighbour, you may call this *wisdom*, but not from above, it is earthly, saith Saint *James*, and which is worse, carnal, sensual and devilish. So that it is plain, the peaceable, meek and patient man. is the wise man, when all is said; for the less patient or meek a man is, the less *wise* he is; *anger* rests in the bosom of *fools*, saith the Preacher, and in the 24 of his *Proverbs* at the *29th* verse he teacheth, that *he that is slow to anger is of great understanding; but he that is hasty of spirit exalteth folly.* *Meeknesse* then is a *vertue* well-becoming a *wise man*.

Jam.3.15.

Eccle.7.9.

Pro.14.29

Secondly

Secondly, It is an *ornament* to the *valiant*, for rafhnefs and fury, and revenge, do rather become a fiend of Hell, than a man who is a creature fitted for fociety. The Heathens could fay it was the *mark* of a poor fpirit to be touch'd with injuries: but a *generous* and *noble mind* did trample and contemn them. And therefore let no man fay that *Meek-neffe* is a want of courage, indeed the *Philofopher* faith, that *anger* is the fpur of *valor*, the whetftone of courage. But the greateft *Philofopher* that ever was, & beft feen in *morals* in the 16. of his *Proverbs* thus fets down. *He that is flow to anger, is better than the mighty: and he that ruleth his fpirit than he that taketh a City.*

No man, I dare fay: will fay that *David* was a *coward*: he was a *fword-man* with a witnefs; a braver **Champion**, a ftouter man of his hands, and of a more valiant *courage* did never
tread

Magni au-tem animi eft propri-um, pla-cidum effe tranquil-lamque at-que injuri-as atque offenfiones fem per de-fpicere. Sen. de Ch. lib. 1. cap. 5. Magni a-nimi eft injurias defpicere, Sen. de ira lib. 2. 32. Pro. 16. 32

tread on Gods earth : for he fought when all *Iſrael* fear'd ; yet *David* was a Meek and tender-hearted man.

Pſa.22.14 My *heart is like wax* (ſaith he) *it is melted in the midſt of my bowels,* yea when that foul-mouth'd *Shemei* revi-

2 Sam.16 7. Ibid.11. 12. led and curſed *David* to his face: yet he forbad to touch him: let him a-lone ; and let him curſe ; *It may be that the Lord will look upon mine affli-ction : and that the Lord will requite good for his curſing this day.* And when *Saul* who ſought after his life, and would be appeas'd by none of his good ſervices, when nothing would ſatisfie the *Tyrant* but the *blood* of that innocent ; and when God had delivered him into *Davids* hand; and his friends and followers perſwaded to *kill* him, yet *David* would not

1 Sam:24. 6. conſent any violence ſhould be of-fer'd him. Yea he was ſo loath at any time to take *offence,* and ſo un-willing to give any , that his

heart

heart fmote him becaufe he had cut off *Sauls skirt*, furely then! it doth not bewray a want of courage to forbear revenge: *Potuiffe nocere & nolle magna eft gloria.* It is the greateft honor that can be to a man, to let pafs occafions of *revenge*, and every good man will account it his glory to pafs by *offences*, and not like many in our daies, who will not fuffer the leaft *injurie* to pafs unrevenged, and for meer *trifles*, grow out of meafure fo *offended*, that the tedious trouble and charge of many years *fuit* can hardly reconcile them.

And others will redeem the leaft difgrace with a ftream of blood, and cannot reft, but like men out of their wits take on, until they fee their enemy weltering in his gore. *Corpore trunco invidiofa dabit minimus folatia fanguis.* Yea moreover to fome, all company is loathfome, all places irkfome, and their own life becomes

1 Sam. 24. 5.

Pro. 19. 11

Quorum præcordia nullis interdum aut levibus videas flagrantia caufis

At vindi-
Et ı lo uum
vita ju-
cundius
ip a.

becomes cumberfome; except they can be avenged of their enemy.

For being *wrong'd* in their *reputa-tion* they take themfelves bound in point of *honor* to repair their *credit* with the life of their Adverfary.

How this will hold with the rules of *Scripture* and of Chriftian *Religion;* let any man who is throughly ac-quainted with either, judg ; where-as indeed in the judgment of the more civil *Heathen* : this practice is reputed *barbarous* : there are other waies for men to right themfelves; and repair their honor allowable both by the *lawes* of God and Man, this of *duel* and fingle *combat* is not. No Man fhould dare in fuch a Cafe to be his own Carver, and to ufurp Gods office ; who by himfelf or his Mini-fters doth undertake to right all fuch as fuffer wrong. He that drawes his *fword* in a private quarrel: unlefs it be to defend himfelf, and to fecure.

his

his own life; Is a *Rebel* againſt heaven; and no color or pretence whatſoever can quit him from bloodguil-
tineſs. I ſhall need to ſay no more
to this purpoſe, ſeeing it ſo clearly
appeares that *Meekneſſe* may vvell
conſiſt vvith *Wiſdom* and *Valour*, and
he is neither *wiſe* nor *valiant* that is
not *meek*. It is a ſeemly *ornament*
for all perſons, and all profeſſions.
And therefore put on Meekneſs in
Ornamentum as the faireſt *ornament* of
a Chriſtian.

Fourthly, in *Monumentum*, a fourth
uſe of *Apparel* it ſerves for *diſtincti-*
on, not of *Sexes* only, but of *call-*
ings. So *Meekneſſe* is the *badg* of
our profeſſion, the *Livery* or cog-
nizance of our *Chriſtian Religion*:
by this (ſaith Chriſt,) *ſhall all men know*
that you are my Diſciples if you love Joh. 13. 35
one another. And therefore Chriſt Joh. 10.
calleth his followers *ſheep*, which is a
gentle, quiet and harmleſs Creature,
and

Mat. 10 16 and *Doves* which is an innocent,
Mat. 18. 3. Meek and gaule-leſs *Creature*. And
Mat 19. *little Children* ſimple without all
13, 14. drifts or aimes.   And Saint *Paul* to
the Romans affirmes that he that hath
Joh. 21. 5. not the ſpirit of *Chriſt* is none of *his*,
Rom 8. 9. now no diſgrace doth touch a man ſo
nere as to ſay he is none of *Chriſts*,
no *Chriſtian*; & no *Chriſtian* he is (St.
Paul tels us) that hath not the ſpirit
of *Chriſt*, now *Chriſts* ſpirit is a ſpirit
Mat. 11. of Meekneſs, *Matth.* 11. 29. *Learn*
29. *of me* (ſaith he) *for I am meek*, ſo!
Meek a man muſt be, or a Chriſtian
he cannot be: or if in name yet not
in deed : for a *Chriſtian* Man is a
Meek Man.

   Thoſe unquiet and turbulent ſpirits, that like *Cadmus* Brethren are
ſo enrag'd againſt one another, that
they cannot reſt whilſt they can ſee
one alive, do ſhew of what generati-
on they are, the ſeed of the Serpent;
by their malicious cruelty they do de-
clare

clare from whence they are defcended; as the *Thiftle* is known by its *pricks,* having nothing notable, either *beauty* or *fweetnefs* to commend it; it would be trod upon without notice but that it difcovereth it felf by *vexing* thofe that touch it.

It is nothing to fee *Creatures* of a favage nature to tear one another: how ill would it become *fheep* of the fame fold; *Doves* of the fame houfe, to put on cruelty and devour one another. And will it not hold as well for Chriftians of the fame profeffion, the refemblance is Chrifts own; thofe men are like wolves and Tygers and fnarling Dogs, (not *Doves and Lambs*) that are clothed with immanity.

Wrath and Cruelty and Quarrelling is a blemifh to the profeffion of *Chriftianity:* for he that profeffes the Chriftian Religion (faith *Socrates* in the feventh Book and fifteenth

M   Chapter

Chapter of his Ecclesiastical history)
ought to be a stranger altogether,
(that is clearly free) from fighting &
quarrelling, and all of the like sort.

Etiam omnino ab his qui quæ Christi unt sapiunt, aliena sunt cædes, pugnæ, & quæ alia sunt hujusmodi. Socrat. *Eccl. hist. lib.* 7. *cap.* 15.

And *Ambrose* in his second Tome
the fift Book of his Orations in the
32. Epistle, doth thus purge himself of his pretended *rebellion* against
the *Emperour*, when I am compel'd
unto it, I am yet to learn what kind
of resistance I shall make. I have
learn'd to sorrow, I can weep, I can
sigh against armed enemies, Soldi-

Coactus repugnare non novi, dolere potero, potero flere, potero gemere adversus arma, milites Gothos quoque lacrymæ meæ arma sunt, talia enim munimenta sunt Sacerdotis, aliter nec debeo, nec possum resistere. Ambr. Tom. 2. *lib.* 5. *orat. in Ep.* 32. *pag.* 123.

ers

ers and *Gothes,* alfo, my tears are my
weapons: It is meet that fuch fhould
be the fortification of one of my profeffion, otherwife I ought not, I cannot refift. The *Chriftian* (faies *Tertullian,*) is no mans foe, we render
to no man evil for evil. We are for-
bidden to wifh evil, to do evil, to
fpeak evil, to think evil of any one
without exception.

*chrifti-
anus nul-
lius eft ho-
fti.* Tert.
*ad Scapu.
cap. 2.
pag. 130.*

*ibid cap. 4. pag. 131. Nulli malum pro malo reddimus, male
enim velle, male facere, male dicere, male cogitare de quoquam
ex æquo vetamur.* Tert. *Apol. adverf. Gentes. cap. 36. pag. 66.
Si malum malo difpungi penes nos liceret, &c.* Tert. *Apol.
adverfus Gentes. cap. 37. per totum.*

   For if it were lawful to return e-
vil for evil, or to wipe out one injury with another, they were abundantly furnifhed with all neceffaries,
both to *defend* themfelves, and *offend*
their enemies, they wanted neither
Men nor *Arms,* number nor force
fufficient: but that they were re-
ftrain'd by the confcience of their
Religion which taught *magis occidi*

liceret

liceret quam occidere. We muſt lay
down the *ſword*, and take up the
Croſs and follow *Chriſt.* I have ſome-
where read of a *Biſhop* of *France* taken (in the wars) a priſoner by the
*King,*unto whom the *Pope* directed a
threatning letter,commanding to ſet
him at liberty, and withal, expoſtu-
lating how *he* durſt violently detain
a ſon of the *Church,* unto whom the
King returned a modeſt *Anſwer,* and
withal,ſent him the *Armour* the *Biſhop* was taken in, with this Inſcripti-
on, *Anne hac eſt tunica filii tui?* does
the *Church* give ſuch liveries to her
Children?

    The *Liverie* of the *Church* of
Chriſt is *Meekneſs*: and the good
Chriſtian is far from brables, and
will rather *ſuffer* evil than *do* any.

*Accipere
quam facere præstat injuriam.* M. T. C. *Tuſc. quæſt. lib.* 5.
φανερὸν δὲ ᾗ ὅτι ἄμφω μὲν φαῦλα, ᾗ τὸ ἀδικεῖσθαι, ᾗ
τὸ ἀδικεῖν. τὸ μὴ γὰρ ἔλαττον, τὸ δὲ πλέιον ἔχειν ἐςὶ
τῆ μέσε. *Ariſt. Ethic. lib.* 5. *cap.* 11.

                           And

And it is more comfort to a Christian and honor too to *suffer* wrong,
than in preventing it or removing it
to *do* wrong. A care therefore should
be had that in seeking ease from the
evil of *punishment*, men burden not
themselves with the *evil of sin*. For
the lightest *sin* is a greater evil than
the heaviest *punishment* in the judg-
ment of the Apostle, *He that doth e-*   Rom. 3.8.
vil that good may come of it, his dam-
nation is just. Now to sin to avoid
a punishment, is to do a *great evil* for
a *little good*: much like to him, who
troubled with a pinching shooe, doth
pare his foot.

Christian men must bear the reproaches and injuries of the men of
the world, their *hearts* must not rise,
nor their *tongues* rail, nor their *hands*
violently attempt any thing against
their enemies: but they must fairly
and gently lay their faults before
them, that they may see their error

and repent of it : and if they will not be reformed, *lawful remedies* when they can be had, may be used; and in the mean time they are to be pityed and prai'd for, till they can be brought to a sober reckoning; and this is the *Meek mans way*, and by this he is known to be what indeed he is, an *honest man*, and a *good Christian*.

But can any man think, or will any man say the *four faces*, the disfigured *countenances*, the rude *behaviour*, uncivil *carriage*, and railing *speeches*, cholerick *fumes*, resisting the truth, men of corrupt minds, no judgment, little honesty, whose folly is manifest to all men, are these the *markes* whereby *Chrijts sheep* are known? or must such fellows as these carry away the note of perfection, whilst all sober men, and all others besides themselves, must lie under the rubbish of a sinful condition ?

these

2 Tim. 3. 8

These kindle the *coales* of contention, throw about their *fire-brands*, fly
in the faces of all that contradict
them, clamour against *Magistracy* and
Ministry with open mouth, as *Jannes*
& *Jambres* resisted *Moses*, so do they ;
they despise dominion, speak evil
of dignities, raging waves of the sea,
foming out their own shame, mur-
murers, complainers, crying down
Ministers, *Sabbaths*, *Sacraments*,
Churches, all *Order* and *Government*
(as the *Edomites* did *Hierusalem*)
raze it, *raze* it even to the foundation thereof. And of these men there
are different *sects*, but although they
have their *heads* turned diverse waies,
and be divided in their *judgments*
and *opinions*, yet like *Samsons foxes*,
they are tied together by the *tailes*,
and in their *ends* and *aimes* they all
agree.

Is this the effect and fruit of that
Third Testament, that *law of love*, that

M 4   *eternal*

Margin notes:
2 Tim. 3. 8

Jude 8.
Jud 8. 13,
16.

Ps. 137. 7.

Judg. 15.
4.

eternal Goſpel (as they are pleas'd to call it) the product of the *holy Ghoſt* in theſe laſt daies ? as theſe *Phanaticks* dream, but I leave theſe vain men.

It is a ſad thing to conſider what ſtirs and broils there have been in the *Chriſtian* world for very trifles : unto what *height* and *heat* the contention has grown amongſt perſons of note and eminency for learning and piety about things of little moment, which would never have been, had there been *Meekneſſe* : for where *Meekneſſe* is, there will be a *quietneſſe* of heart, a calmneſs of *ſpirit,* a *teachableneſſe,* a *tractableneſſe,* an *eaſineſſe* to be perſwaded, there will be *patience, humility,* and a fear and *tenderneſſe* of offending.

For want of *Meekneſſe* what lamentable *rents* have been in the *Church* of Chriſt in former times : not only about things *indifferent,* (the
Eaſterne

Eafterne Church following one cuftom & the *Wefterne* another, oppofing each other with great bitternefs).

But alfo about things meerly *miftaken,* the contention has grown fo hot between the Greek and *Latin Churches,* that the *Chriftian* world was like to be torn in peeces for a miftake of words: the *Greeks* judging the Latins *Sabellians*: and the *Latins* the Greeks *Arrians*: had not this difference been feafonably compos'd by *Athanafius.*

In latter times what contentions have arifen in the Churches of *Germany, Sweden, Denmark, France, Helvetia,* about the ubiquitarie prefence, predeftination, lofing and not lofing of grace, &c. Which were much encreafed by *writing* and *diſputing,* that might have happily been ended by a friendly *Mediation,* if in a meek way the *meaning* of both parties had been throughly fifted.

And

Read *Euſ.* and *Soc.* their Ecclefiafti-cal hiftories.

And in these latter daies what fearful *rents* have been, and are still a-mongst us, he has *no mind* that *considers* not: no *heart* that *condoles* not: *Quis talia fando temperet a lacrymis?* who can keep the Rivers of tears within the banks of their eyes? whose heart doth not bleed, whose spirit is not broken, (and who in the anguish of his soul, could not wish each pore of his body, an eye; that every eye might weep, for brinish bloody tears) when he seriously thinks of the miserable distractions that are amongst us? the land is di- _{Psa.60.2.} vided, Lord heal the sores of it, for it shaketh. Oh could we but right-ly lay to heart the mischiefs of our divisions, how *odious* to God; how *pernitious* to Religion. Alas that the *Church* of Christ should be so *rent* about certain *accidentals*, *imma-terials*, *unnecessaries*: when there is agreement in *fundamentals* and such points

)oints as are *essential* to salvation ; a-
way with thofe *contentions* that occafion *shame* and *loss* to both fides.
And let us endeavour to quench
thofe *flames* which have already
burnt down fo many and fo worthy
parts of the houfe of God.

When *Meeknesse* hath been laid
afide, and cruelty put on, what lamentable combuftions have been in
the Chriftian World? what fury did
Sathan fend up, to animate Nation?a-
gainft Nation : and in the fame Nation one man againft another; the
mifchiefs o f an inteftine Warre (occafion'd for want of *Meeknesse*) the
Ruines of *Germany* evidently fpeak,
and I would I might have *fought* an
inftance at fo great a diftance, and
not *found* one nearer home, even
in the bowels of this *Kingdom*,
What *divifions* have there been ?
What *feditions* have been mov'd ?
What *fractions* have been rais'd ?
The

The gliftering *fword*, whofe face flafhes forth lighting of *terror*, hath paffed through the land, wafting and deftroying : the fad Calamities of a *Civil Warre* are better known than that I fhould fpend time to repeat them.

Alas! what hath any *Kingdome* gain'd at any time by this way, befides *fpilling* the blood, and *fpoiling* the goods of the unhappy people. And it terrifieth me to Remember how many flourifhing *Empires* and *Kingdomes*, have been by means of fuch Contentions, either torn in peeces with inteftine divifion, or fubdued to forrain Princes, under pretence of affiftance and aid! And our own *Chronicles* make mention how fore this Kingdom hath been fhaken with thefe dangerous evils,

The Barons wars, and the wars between the Houfes of *Yorke* and *Lancafter*.

And

And yet neither the examples of o-
ther Countries, nor miseries of their
own are sufficient to make men beware; and you shall ever observe it
of any Nation, that then it *begins*
to be *miserable*, when it *ceases* to
be *obedient*. *Rebellion* puts an end to
the *prosperity*, and gives beginning
to the *misery* of any people.

πειθαρχία ἐϛι της ἐυπραξίας μέτρ. ἐυεργέτησι γὸ ἐι ὄρ-
χοντες μεγάλως τας πολεις, διὰ γὸ ἀυτῶν ὁ βιὸς ἡμων συνίϛατι.
Theophilact. *Com. in Ep. ad* Rom. 13. 1.

Let us then beseech the God of
mercy that he would send down
from Heaven a spirit of *Meeknesse,*
and raise up on earth able and fit
Instruments to make up the *breaches,*
and to quiet the *distractions* that are
amongst us, to cure the *wounds* and
heale the hurt of the Daughter of his Jer. 6. 14.
People.

For let me tell the World, tedious *suites* and bloody *Warres* are

a

a scandal to the *Christian Riligion.*
It were a great deale more comely
(thinks our Apoſtle) to put on
Meekneß, to ſuffer wrong, and to

1 Cor. 6. 7. ſuſtain harm. Yet I would not be
miſtaken, as if my meaning were to
deprive men of the benefit of that
means which God hath ordained to

Rom. 13. 2 right ſuch as are wronged , for the
Magiſtrate is the *Miniſter* of Gods
ordinance.

For the preſervation of mens
lives, honors and eſtates : as well by
force of Arms, as *ſuites* of law.

Yet no *ſuite of law* muſt be com-
menced but with Meekneſs, in love
& charity : no *wars* begun but by the
Command of a lawful *Authority.*
And in both, in *ſuits* of law & *feats* of
Arms, juſtice, not mallice muſt
bear the ſway : and not the fury of
unruly *paſsion,* but the wholſome
direction of rectified *reaſon* ſhould
govern our *affaires.* The *Lord of*
Hoaſts

Hoaſts is the *God of peace* , and thither ſhould ſuites and war tend, to gain a more ſafe, honorable and ſetled peace.

A *Chriſtian* man ſhould ſtudy to be quiet, his deſire and his endeavour both ſhould be for quietneſs and peace, *If it be poſsible as much as in you lies,live peaceabliewith all men* : But if men will be ſo quarrelſome, ſo froward and contentious, that nothing will perſwade them to *peaceableneſs* : and that our cauſe is much like that of *Davids*, to dwell amongſt thoſe that are enemies to peace, that when we ſpeak of peace they are for warre. If we do what in us lies, and what is poſſible for us to do, and yet they will not be quiet, nor abate any thing of their ſavage nature, we may implore the aid of heaven, and pray the *God of peace* to aſſiſt us againſt the *Enemies of peace*, and

Rom. 12, 18.

Pſ.120 7.

and then let God ariſe and let his e-
nemies be ſcattered; let them alſo
that hate him, flee before him.

In perſwading to *Meekneſſe* then,
the Apoſtle never meant to deprive
men of lawful *remedies* againſt *wrongs*
and *injuries,* when in a fair way with
moderation and *Meekneſſe* men ſeek
to right themſelves. But only to let
men know how well it becometh
Chriſtian men to be gentle & mild,
& to proſecute their affaires not with
rigour and ſeverity, but with *Meekneſſe,* by ſuch proceedings giving
men to underſtand that reformation,
not revenge is aim'd at.

And as this is the proper *garb of a
Chriſtian,* ſo amongſt Chriſtians it

beſt becometh $\left\{ \begin{array}{c} \text{Magiſtrates} \\ \text{and} \\ \text{Miniſters.} \end{array} \right.$

Mildneſß doth well become a *Chriſtian*

tian Magiſtrate, who ſhould order his
actions according to Reaſon, not
after his Paſſion. Clemencie (faith
Symeſius) is βασιλικώτατην, a vertue meet
for a Prince, whoſe royal diſpoſition
is better known by gracious remiſſi-
ons, than rigorous exactions. The
Orator praiſing *Caſar,* above all, commends him for his *Clemencie,* that
his fortune had nothing greater than
that he had power, his nature nothing better, than that he had will
to ſave many; and the Philoſopher
doth not only commend, but even
admire the rare temper of that Prince,
who importuned by one of his Of-
ficers to ſubſcribe a Bill againſt certain malefactors, after ſome delayes,
being urged to ſigne the writing, he
much againſt his will, took the pa-
per, and cried out, *I would I knew*

*Nihil eſt
tam popu-
lare quam
bonitas:
nulla de
virtutibus
tuis plʋri-
mis nec
gratior nec
admirabi-
lior miſe-
recordia,
nihil habet
fortuna tua
majus qam
ut poſſis :
nec natura
tua melius
quam ut*

velis. conſervare quam plurimos. Cicero *Orat. vol.* 3. *in Orat.
pro Ligario in fine.*

*Invitus invito cum chartam protuliſſet traderetque excla-
maſti vellem neſcire literas. Sen. in lib.* 2, *de Clem. c.* 1.

N   *not*

not how to write. And *Theodosius* the younger, when it was demanded of him why he would not punish some capital offences, made answer, *I would it were in my power to restore life to the dead.*

utinam mihi liceret, & mortuos ad vitam revocare.

And the clemencie of those Magistrates is worthy to be remembred, who deferred the execution of *such persons* (that by their Lawes were condemned to die) for certain dayes, that in the interim enquiry might be made, whether any thing could be found in favour of them, that they might be spared.

Moses the best *Magistrate* that ever was, was the *meekest* man that ever was; and it is written of the *Kings of Israel*, that they were *merciful Kings.* *Magistrates* are Gods upon earth, and it cannot be denied but they are the best Magistrates that come nearest to the example of God; now God is loving to every one

Num. 12. 3.

1 Kin. 20. 3

Psal. 82. 6.

one, and *his tender mercies are over all his works.* The Bees (it is said) amongst themselves do exercise a certain *discipline,* and have the forme of a *Common-wealth,* and amongst them there is a Master *Bee,* whom all the rest do follow as their *King,* yet this Bee is without a *sting;* even nature teaches the chief *Magistrate* to be gentle and gracious, and it will turn much to his advantage, for in being such, he shall be more *safe,* more *honoured,* and better *obeyed.*

Psa.145.9.

Insignis Regis forma, dissimilisq; cæteris tum magnitudine, tum nitore hoc tamen maxime distinguitur iracundissimæ & pro corporis captu pugnacissi-

-mæ sunt apes, & acculeos in vulnere relinquunt: Rex ipse sine aculeo est, noluit illum natura nec sævum esse, n°c ultionem magno constitutam petere: telumque detraxit, & iram ejus inermem reliquit. Sen. de Clem. lib. 1. cap. 19.

1. More *safe* he shall be, the *peoples love is the Princes greatest safety,* and this is procured, and maintained with gentlenesse and humanity, the wisest and the greatest *Princes* have

Regibus certior est ex Mansuetudine securitas. Sen. de Clem. lib. cap. 8.

Vnum est inexpugnabile munimentum, amor, civium. Sen. de Cle. lib. 1. cap. 19.,   N 3   left

*Qui Cle-
mentes fue-
rè maxima
ex parte
usque, ad
seros annos
tuto vixe-
runt. Bapt.
Campoful.
in lib. 5.
exempl.
Illius mag-
nitudo sta-
bilis, fun-
dataque
est, quem
omnes tam
supra se
esse quam
prose sci-
unt. Sen.
de Clem.
lib. 1. cap. 3*

left to the world many notable examples of their *Clemencie,* whereby
they have established their *throne,* and
made their *Empires* more firme and
lasting, *illius magnitudo stabilis fun-
dataque est,* his *Majesty* is sure and
permanent whom men are perswad-
ed is for them as well as above them,
who watches for their welfare, whose
presence begets in his subjects a *love*
as well as *reverence,* not flying from
him, but running to him as to an *A-
sylum* or Sanctuary; such an one they
ought to esteem as the breath of
their nostrils, worth ten thousand of
themselves.

2. He shall be more *honoured* for
his *Clemencie,* it is the most precious
Jewel in the *Crowns* of *Princes,* an
addition to their greatnesse, hath in
it a *majesty* as well as *sweetnesß,* which
not allures only, but awes. A *Clement Prince* is an object for *love* and
wonder to stand amazed at, unto
whom

whom all men *tanquam ad Clarum ac beneficum fidus certatim advolant,* can there be a greater honour than was that of *Titus,* to be the *darling* of the world ? What can be more honourable , than to live with the good liking of all ? whofe life is tendered as a common benefit of *mankind,* whofe death is the fear of al, the hope of none, whofe prefence is defired as fome *Cœleftial influence,* and whofe perfon is beheld with almoft a divine *veneration,* for he that comes neareft to God in his *clemencie* and moderation, why fhould he not be next to God in our love and eftimation?

Titus cognomine paterno amor ac deliciæ humani generis. C. Suetoni. Tran. de vita Titi. vefp. 12. Cæfar.quid pulchrius quam vi- v re optantibus cunctis. Sen de Clem. lib. 1.c.19.

3. He fhall be *better obey'd* : Rigour and feverity is an *unfafe* and an *unpleafant* way to keep the people in their obedience. Man is a fociable creature , and is eafilyer led , than drawn. The will of man is fooner tamed with *advis'd* following , than

Verecundi-
am peccan-
di, facit
ipsa Cle-
mentia re-
gentis. S.n.
de Clem.
lib. 1. c. 22.
R *missius*
imperanti
melius pi-
retur. Sen.
de Clem.
lib. 1. c. 24.

rash resisting.   Besides the clemencie of the Magistrate makes the subject ashamed to offend, for he must
needs be accounted extremely bad,
whom a *Magistrate* inclined to *pity,*
doth *punish.*   Therefore the saying
of the Philosopher is to be approv'd,
who saith, *The people will be best ru-*
led, when they are mildly governed.
Yet a care must be had that the *Ma-*
gistrate be not too *remiß* in punish-
ing, for some if they shall perceive
the *reins* of government to be slack-
ened like a mettal'd *horse,* they will
overthrow the R*ider.*   It is better
to live under a rigid *government*
where no man dare do any thing,
than in an *Anarchie,* where any man
dare do all things.   It is likely to
go ill with the *good,* when *bad* men

Principis
erga scele-
ratos len'-
tas, est in
bonos cru-
deltas. Cic.
3 *offic.*

may do what they will; clemencie
to the bad, is cruelty to the good: it
is the duty of a good *Magistrate* to
stop the mouth of *wickednesse,* and to
                                    vindicate

vindicate a wronged *innocencie.* The discreet Magistrate will wisely distinguish, he will ‖make a difference, that *honest* men be not *discouraged,* and the hands of the *wicked strengthened.*

When *wickednesse* is grown *exemplary,* and wickd men incorrigible, the Magistrate must deal with them as the Chirurgeon with an unsound *member,* cut it off lest it endanger the whole body; for it is better that one *member* perish, than that the whole body should be *ruin'd, the safety of many is to be preferred before the pleasure of one :* " seasonable justice prevents many mischiefs, which after " knows no remedy but patience; " *lenity* in some cases is *cruelty.*

But as the *Chirurgeon* in cutting off a *member,* or searching of a *wound,* is deaf to the *complaints* of his patient, and heeds not his *teares* nor his *cries,* till he have done his work. So

Immedicabile vulnus ense recidendum, ne pars sincera trahatur Quia melius est paucorum supplicio universos eximi quam in omnes vindicari. Ambrof.

the

the *good* Magiſtrate, though never ſo *meek,* doth ſtop his eares to the *cries* of the *guilty :* It is for *women* and *children* to be mov'd with the *teares* and *ſufferings* of deſperate and incorrigible offenders.

The Magiſtrate then is *meek* and *merciful,* not, that puniſheth not at all ; but with juſtice and due moderation, and that having juſt cauſe to puniſh, hath reſpect both to the meaſure, and to the end. Reſpect muſt be had to the meaſure, for ſome there are who having *cauſe* to puniſh, know no *mean* in puniſhing, but proceed to that height that mans nature is diſhonour'd in a perſonal ſuffering.

Aⁱus & *muliercula* *ſunt, qua* *lachrimis* *nocentiſſi-* *morum mo-* *ventur.* Senec. de Clem. *lib.* 2. cap. 5 *Aut ut eum* *quⁱempunit,* *emendt :* *aut ut pæ* *na ejus cæ-* *teros meli-* *o ſreddat:* *aut ut ſub-* *latis malis* *ſecurioⁱes* *cæteri vi-* *vant.* Sen. de Clen. *lib.* 1. *cap.* 22.   *Cⁱudeles ſunⁱ quⁱ puⁱⁱndi cauſam ba-* *benⁱ, moⁱum non habⁱnⁱ.* Sen. de Clem. *lib.* 2. cp. 4.

2. Reſpect muſt be had to the *end,* and that is, firſt the reformation, not deſtruction of the delinquent:

quent : for a difference muſt be made between the ſin and the ſinner , the perſon and his fault ; let the fault be corrected, but let the perſon be ſpared, and ſo puniſh, that the ſin may be deſtroyed, and the ſinner ſaved.

A ſecond end of puniſhing the *guilty*, is for the example of others, that they may fear and beware leſt they fall into the ſame condemnation, *jungantur in culpa non ſeparentur in pœna.* It is the rule of juſtice that they who are guilty of the ſame offence, ſhould partake of the ſame puniſhment.

A third end of puniſhing, is that the evil being removed and taken out of the way, the reſt may live the more ſecurely ; for when the wicked periſh, the righteous encreaſe, *Prov.* 28.28.

Pro.28.28.

For as the painful *husbandman* doth gather out the *weeds* that the *Corne* may *grow* the better, and *cuts* off

off the superfluous and dead *branches* of his *trees* and *vines,* that they may bear *fruit* the better; so doth the *good Magistrate* deal with such men, whom he shall find to be *pernicious* and *unprofitable* to the *Common-wealth.*

And thus as *Justice* hath respect unto the *cause,* so hath *Clemencie* regard unto the *measure,* and to the *end;* for the *Magistrate,* like the Surgeon, should have an *Eagles* eye, a *Lions heart,* but a *Ladies* hand; *skill* and *courage,* but withal *tendernesse* and *gentlenesse.*

For the threats of the Magistrate should be like *thunder,* which affrights many with the *noise,* hurts few with the *stroke,* and therefore the Magistrate hath the sword carried before him in the sheath (*ferrum vagina reconditum*) and is not to be drawn but upon weighty occasion, they must be sparing of blood, even of the most vile.

Clementia sua severitatem sententiæ temperavit. Hieron.*in Lucam.*18.27. *Vt fulmina paucorum periculo cadunt,omnium metu; sic animadversions magna um potestatum terrent latius quam nocent.* Sen de Clem. lib.1.c. 8. *Summa parsimonia etiam vilissimi sanguinis.* Sen. de Clem. lib. 1.cap. 1.

now you have heard that
a *garment* meet for the
wear.

y, mildneſſe doth well be-
iniſter; the Prophet ſaith
ou Lord art good and gra-
of great kindneſſ to all   Pſal.86.5.
on thee. Rigour and ſe-
ill become the ſervant
rd is gentle and full of
he Miniſters of the Go-
be followers of Chriſt,
Lamb for *meekneſſe* : for
ſter never ſo well gifted,
tongue of men and An-
have not *meekneſſe* and
nothing ; and therefore   1 Cor. 13. 1
advice is, *let all things be*   1 Cor. 16
: and his *practice* was   14.
r them with whom he
, the people under his
gently did he handle
kindly did he entreat   2 Cor. 10. 2
ſt them : praying them :   2 Cor. 2. 8
exhorting   2 Cor. 6. 1.

exhorting them with all earneſtneſs,
beſeeching them ; and ſo often as he
ſpeaks unto them, it is in all tender-
derneſſe as a father to his children ;
in all things ſo behaving himſelf,
that his care towards them in the
ſight of God might appear.

When a point of *doctrine* is to be
delivered,he will have that done with
a *kind affection* , follow the truth in
love : when *ſin* is to be *reproved* ,
that muſt be done in *tender compaſſion. I have often told you, and now tell
you weeping.*

When any *abuſe* is to be *reformed,* he will have it done with a *gentle
moderation* ; *If any man be overtaken
with a fault , ye which are ſpiritual
reſtore ſuch an one with the ſpirit of
meekneſſe : And we were gentle a-
mongſt you* (ſaith the Apoſtle) *even
as a nurſe cheriſheth her children* ; for
a *nurſe* to quiet her *infant, cum dabit verbera, oſtendit ubera,* ſhews the
breaſts,

2Cor.10.1

2Cor.6.13

2Cor.7.12

Eph.4.15.

Phil.3.18.

Gal.6.1.

1Theſ.2.7

breaſts, when ſhe ſhakes the *rod*. Saint *Paul* to the *Corinthians*, the firſt *Ep.* the fourth *Chapter*, at the laſt *verſe*, *Shall I come unto you* (ſaith he) *with the rod, or in love, and in the Spirit of meekneſſe*; for the *good* Miniſt r, like *Davids ſhepheard*, hath a *rod* as well as a *ſtaffe*. A *rod* of correction, as well as a *ſtaff* of conſolation; A *ſtaffe* to uphold the *weak*, a *rod* to beat down the *wicked*. For the Miniſter, if occaſion be, may, and ought to uſe ſharpneſſe , according to the power which the Lord hath given to *edification*, and not to *deſtruction*.

    When *Chriſt* was transfigured on the mount, there appeared with him *Moſes* and *Elias*. *Moſes* the giver of the *Law*, the meekeſt man alive. *Elias* a revealer of the *Goſpel*, a man full of zeal and fervencie. The ſeverity of the Law required a gracious diſpencer ; and therefore it was given in the hand of a *Mediator*; but
                          the

1 Cor. 4. ult.

Pſal. 23.

2 Cor. 13. 10.

the Grace of the Goſpel requires a zealous Miniſter.

The Word of God is a *precious treaſure*, but the *Miniſters* of this Word are but *earthen veſſels*, men of like infirmities and paſſions with your ſelves (as Saint *Paul* ſaid) we have this treaſure in earthen veſſels, and as the liquor reliſhes of the veſſel, ſo amidſt the divine graces of the holy Spirit, *aliquid humani intervenit*, there is ſome reliſh of humane paſſions and affections; hence we ſee ſome of Gods ableſt ſervants, his beſt Miniſters, ſometimes too paſſionate and haſty, and ſometimes too remiſſe and ſlow: and therefore as the ſlow are to be excited and quickened, ſo are the haſtie to qualifie their natural ſharpneſſe with gentleneſſe and moderation. *Peter* was a mild man, *filius Jona,* the ſonne of a Dove, and therefore had *James* and *John* joyn'd with him who were *Boanerges,*

nerges, fonnes of thunder.

Paul on the other fide was of a ta't and fharp nature, and had for his companion, *Barnabas*, a fon of confolation.

The Minifter of the Word, hath a word of terror for the obftinate and ftubborne, a word of comfort for fuch as are poor and penitent; to the one he comes like *Elias* in a *whirlwind* to beat him down; to the other he comes like *Noahs Dove*, with the *O-live branch* of peace in his mouth to raife him up : to the one he is the *favour of death unto death* : to the other *of life unto life.*

Yet whatever their condition be, the *Minifter* of the *Gofpel* is to preach *Repentance*, and to offer *Grace* to all that will accept it, and this is to be done with all *gentleneffe*, for the will of man is naturally ftubborne, and therefore *fweetly* to encline it, and *gently* to move it, is the beft means *effectu-*

*Natura con-
tumax eft
humanus
animus,
& in con-
trarium at-
que arduum
nitens : fe-
quiturque
facilius
quam du-
citur. Sen.
de Clem.
lib.1.c.2.*
2 Pet. 3.9.
1 Tim.2.4.
Ez 33.11.
Ez.18.23.
Joel.2.13.
Mat. 5.48.
1Pet.5.10.

effectually to perswade it, which o-
therwise will become *invincible* by
any terrors or threats of death or
judgment, there is no more ready
way to snatch a man out of the hand
of sin, and to make him willing to
run the way of Gods Command-
ments, then to preach the Word in
meeknesse, for is not God the *Father,*
the *Father of mercie? not willing that
any should perish, but that all should
come to repentance, who will have all
men to be saved, and to come unto
the knowledge of the truth:* He desires
*not the death of a sinner, but is gra-
cious and merciful, slow to anger, and
of great kindnesse, forgiving sinnes
and iniquities;* and are we not called
to the imitation of our *heavenly Father,* to be like him in this particular,
in *patience and meeknesse, and tendernesse of compassion? God* the *Sonne* is
the *God of all grace,* the very character of *meeknesse,* *who would not*
break

break the bruised reed; nor quench the smoaking flax. Who came not to deftroy mens lives but to fave them. Not to beat down, but to build up the broken-hearted, when he comes it is like dew upon a fleece of wooll, or like rain upon the mown grafs. And the fame mind Saint *Paul* would have in us all, that was in him.

God the *holy Ghoft* he is the *Comforter*, the God of all confolation that breaths inward comfort into the foul, whofe working is very fecret and infenfible, but with great efficacy, powerful, fweet and unfpeakable. The God of love and unity he is, and delights to be where men live in peace and amity, appeared to Chrift in the fhape of a *Dove,* and worketh in all that are Chrifts the properties of a Dove: *meeknefs, gentlenefs, fimplicity and innocency,* and if there were no more, this is fufficient; the united examples of the

O   three

Mat.12.20

Luk.9.56.

Ifa.61.1.

Pfa.72 6.

Phil.2. 5.

Mat.3.

three perſons, *Father*, *Son*, and *holy Ghoſt*, to work us to this gracious practice of *meekneſs* in our callings, and Saint *Paul* ſheweth that the ſervant of the Lord muſt be no *ſtriker*, but gentle towards all men, apt to teach, ſuffering the evill men patiently, *Inſtructing them with meekneſs that are contrary minded, if God at any time will give them repentance that they may know the truth.* It
is ſure our *Tribe* hath met with many diſcouragements, ſtrong oppoſitions, what dealings they have found, let Saint *Luke* ſpeak *Acts* 13. 45. where he brings in the Jews ſpeaking againſt Saint *Paul, contradicting and blaſphemíng, putting from them the word of God, and judging themſeves unworthy of everlaſting life.* Of ſuch the Apoſtle hath paſs'd his ſentence, *he that troubleth you ſhall bear his judgment, whoſoever he be.* VVherefore let Miniſters, who ſuffer according

to

2 Tim.2. 25.

Act.13. 45, 46.

1 S.4. 10.

to the will of God *patiently* wait upon the Lord, and commit themselves
to him in *well doing,* meekly atten-
ding the manifeſtation of that *mercy*
which God will in due time *reveal,* Pro. 22. 23
will plead their *cauſe,* & *ſpoil* the ſoul
of them that *ſpoiled* them. And now
you have heard *Meekneſs* is a *garment*
meet for the *Miniſters* wear.

I aſtly, It is a *Garment* for every mans wear, of what condition ſoever he be; if he be *poor,*
meekneſs will make him patient and
content with his *poverty* ; if he be
rich, meekneſs will make him humble,
and thankful to God for his *wealth* ; if
he be *wiſe* and *learned,* *meekneſs* will
make him *ſober* and *moderate* ; and if
he be given to be *angry, meekneſs* will
make him *diſcreet and temperate,* if
a man have *offended,* *meekneſs* will
make him *penitent,* and if he be *in-*
nocent, *meekneſs* will make him
peaceable and quiet. If a man be *re-*
O 2 *viled,*

viled, injur'd, perſecuted, afflicted,
meekneſs will make him *ſilent*, or
ſpeaking to pity, or to pray for the
ſlanderous and injurious. And if he
be *praiſed*, or honored, *meekneſs*
will make him *modeſt*, gentle, not
proud nor puffed up.

You percieve how much it
concernes every man, in whatſoever condition he is in, to get
meekneſs; which, that he may

do $\begin{cases} \text{ſomewhat he muſt labor for.} \\ \text{ſomewhat he muſt beware of.} \end{cases}$

Of thoſe things he muſt labour
for.

The Firſt is *humility*: For where
humility is, there will be *meekneſs*;
an *humble heart* is the proper habita-
tion of a *meek ſpirit*. He that is
humble will look into himſelf, & un-
derſtanding upon enquiry what a poor
thing

thing himſelf is; will learn to deny himſelf and acknowledg his defects, imperfections, ſinfulneſs, the dangers and miſeries he is liable unto, will have a mean *opinion* of himſelf.

Will not *deſpiſe* or envy men.

Will not *murmure* or repine a-gainſt God.

But will account the meaneſt of Gods mercies too *great*, and too *good* for him, and will be contented with that portion, God in his providence ſhall deal out unto him whatſoever it be.

The Second thing he muſt labour for; is love and *charity*, for where theſe are, there will be *meekneſs*.

If there be any thing ſaid. ⎫
⎬ that
If there be any thing done. ⎭

is capable of a good conſtruction; Charity will give it.

Where

Where there is *Peace* and *Unity;* Charity will seek to maintain them.

Where there are differences and distractions, *Charity* will labour to compose them.

Where any thing is amiss, *Charity* will seek to amend it; for want of which *Charity*, what woful rents and breaches have there been, even amongst Brethren. Witness the falling out between *Paul* and *Barnabas*, *Chrysostome* and *Epiphanius*, between *Hierome* and *Ruffinus*, *Eustathius* and *Eusebius*.

Act. 15. 39

Zozom. Eccl. hist. lib. 8. cap. 15.

Socrat. *Eccl. hist. lib. 6. cap. 14. H i mihi qui vos alicubi, simul invenire non possum, sort · ut nunc nove at --- ne de vobis ea scribendo spargatis, quæ quandoque concordes d l re non poteritis.* Aug. Ep. 15. Zozom. *hist. Eccles. lib. 2. cap. 18.*
Socrat. *Eccl. hist. lib. 1. cap. 24.*

And those hot contentions between the *Lutherans* and *Calvenists*, the *Remonstrants* and *Contraremonstrants*. How have these contentions been heightned and aggravated which

which might have been happily re-conciled, if each fide would have laid afide all prejudice, and met toge-ther in charity with Meeknefs.

Thirdly, Labour for a good *con-fcience*, not *fcrupulous* to take of-fence, but *tender* to give offence.

A *Confcience* mifinformed is a blind guide, fuch, like the *Ponticks* in the Moon light, will fight with their own fhadowes: troublefome they are and unfatisfied; and will be contented with no *Religion*: except fuch as is after the *module* they have fet up in their *addle-heads*. With fome (all unlawful both opinions and practifes fhall go for *Confcience*.) Affection and the ftiffnefs and un-flexiblenefs of their own wils: con-jectures and opinions how are men carried away with, and *Confcience* muft bear out all. Men who never made *Confcience* of any thing, yet if it come to be queftioned, wherein

Per erro-rem longe cadentes umbras fu-as quafi hoftium corpora pe-tebant.

Luc. Flo. de Bel. Pontico.

Ifa. 5 20. i

O 4   they

they are concern'd or intereſted , they will evade a duty ſo far as the pretence of *Conſcience* will ſerve their turn.

Now let any man judg what ef-fects the granting liberty of conſci-ence is likely to produce.

Iſa.5.2c.

Raſhneſs ſhall go for *reſolution* , fa-ction for *zeal, good* for *evil,* & *evil* for *good* ; and groſſeſt abſurdities ſhall be palliated under *Conſcience.*

To inſtance in ſome particulars the conſcience of *truth ,* take *truth* for *religion.* Then the *truth* of *re-ligion* there is nothing more to be laid to *Conſcience.*

Yet that may not paſs for *truth* of *Religion ,* which ſome men will take up and ſtand upon , if it be *funda-mental ,* admit not the variation of a *letter : hold faſt* to it , *recede not* from it , *contend earneſtly* for it.

But if it be otherwiſe , a circum-ſtantial *truth* only , of little mo-ment,

nent, some *logomachia*, some trifle
of small *concernment*, lay not this
to *conscience* : better an unnecessary
rath be lost, than the unity of the
Church, detain not the truth of God
in unrighteousness.

In Ep. Conft. *ad* Alex. *& Arium* - *Num æquum sit ut pro- pter modicas quasdam ac vanas verborum inter nos contentationes frater fratri, &c.* ibid. *Tam exilibus & nullo modo neces- sariis de caufis inter nos dimicamus.* ibid. *aliqua de re lepi- cula.* Rom. 1. 18.

Repute not that *zeal* which is *pas- sion*, in matters of lesser moment,
it is *Christian prudence* to prefer
peace, and far better it is for the glory of God, and edification of the
Church to be quiet than contend.
A man to act according to *conscience* at all times is not *warrantable*;
for *truth*, though it must never be
deni'd, is not alwaies to be *declar'd.*

Besides *God* is above *conscience*,
and God hath set us *Rules* to act by,
and if we leave Gods *Rule* to follow
our

our own *humour*, this some will call *conscience*, but such an one as must first be *mortified*, then *Reform'd*.

And what is more usual than to pretend *conscience*, when other matters are intended. *Hypocrisie* is a *painted Sepulchre*; what is more usual then to paint over a rotten heart with a zealous mouth, *Absolons vow* is his Mask for his *Conspiracy* against *David*, and *Jezabels fast* is heis for destroying *Naboth* ~~Ahab~~. The *Hypocrite* under pretence of *Religion* hath other aimes than Gods service, and only makes *Religion* for which he seems so hot, a *Stalking-horse* to his own ends.

The greatest *villanies* that ever the Sun saw, have been committed under pretence of *Religion* and *Conscience*: What will men be asham'd? What will men be afraid to do? that in a bad cause dare appeal to *God* and *Conscience*; to say nothing of the waiwardnes

See Dr.
Hal.

waiwardneſs of a ſcrupulous and miſ-
informed *conſcience*; all that I ſhall
ſay, is to wiſh all men by all means
to labour to inform their *conſciences*
aright, which will lead them in
their way with *calmneſs and quietneſs*,
get a good *conſcience* and that is the
way to Meekneſs.

Fourthly, Labour for *Unity*, for
where that is, there will be *meekneſs*; this *Unity* is ſpiritual, (ſo St.
Paul cals it) the unity of the ſpirit.
For if one ſpirit do animate all,
and act in all; All will be as the primitive *Chriſtians* were, and as Saint
Paul would have all *Chriſtians* to be,
of one mind and of one heart.

Act. 2. 1.

Where men are divided in their
minds, there is, *diſſention*.

They *think* otherwiſe, and as
they *think*, ſo they *teach*, and *teach*
ſo becauſe they *conſent* not.

Where men are divided in their
hearts, they are eſtranged in their
affections,

1 Tim. 6.
3.

affections, and there is *discord*.

So where there is *division*, there is *dissention* and *discord*.

And what *meeknes* can there be where these are?

Whereas being one in *mind* and *heart*, there will be *Kindnes* and *Gentlenes* to each other, for thus united they will conspire together for the welfare of each other; and will *help* one another, and *forbear* one another, and *bear* with one another, and be kindly *affectionated* one towards another, will *love* one another, and *do good* to one another, for where is *unity*, every one partakes of the *benefit* of any one.

This *spiritual unity* is of *two kinds*:
An *unity of faith*; and,
An *unity of order*.

For thus all joyned together in one by a spiritual *bond* a religious *knot*; (for *Religion* they say comes a *Religando*) because it fastens and ties

all

ill in one: the *body* to the *head*, and
the *members* one to *another*, so the
Apoſtle, *we being many are one body
in Chriſt.* Now of theſe two unities
we ſhall firſt enquire how the unitie
of *faith* tends to *meekneſſe.* That
faith is *one* Saint *Paul* puts it out of
Queſtion, there is but *one faith.*

*Dictam
eſſe Religi-
onem quod
quaſi in
faſcem Do-
mini vin-
cti & reli-
gati ſumus.*
Hieron.
*Diximus
Religionis*

*nomen a vinculo pietatis eſſe deductum; quod hominem ſibi Deus
religaverit & pietate conſtrinxerit.* Lact. *Inſt. lib. 4. cap. 28.*

*Hoc vinculo pietatis obſtricti Deo & religati ſumus, unde
ipſa religio nomen accepit. idem ibid.*

*Religio dicta eſt, eo quod per eam uni ſoli Deo religamus ani-
mas noſtras, ad cultum divinum animo ſerviendi.* Iſidor. *lib.
8. Etym.*

*Religio eſt, qua ſi anima uni Deo unde ſe peccato ſeperave-
rat reconciliatione ligat.* Auguſt. *lib. de quantitate animæ.*

Rom. 12. 5.   1 Cor. 12. 12, 13.   Eph. 4. 5.

For as there is but *one common
ſalvation* that any man can hope for,
So is there but one common *faith*
which every man muſt profeſſe *alike
pretious in all.*

   This faith is *one*, as having *one
divine*

Jude 3.
Tit. 1. 4.
2 Pet. 1. 1.

Joh. 2. 22.
Mar. 1. 15.
2 Theſ. 2.
12, 13.
1 Tim. 4. 3.

Act. 20. 21.
Gal. 2 16.
Gal 3. 26.
Eph. 3. 12,
17.
Rev. 14.
12.
Joh. 11. 27
& 14. 1.
Act. 8 37.
& 16 31.
Joh. 2. 11.
Rom. 3.
26.
1 Joh. 5.
1, 5, 10.

divine truth for the general objɷct of
it.

And *one Lord Jesus Christ* for the
special object of it.

The *general object of faith* which
is the *Gospel* is a *Doctrine of meekness.*

The *special object* of faith (which
is *Christ*) is an example of *meekness.*

So, that where true faith is , there
must necessarily be *meekness.*

For as *faith unites* the soul unto
God by the band and *conscience of Religion* ; so doth it *unite* one to another by the band of *love.*

But where men are divided in
their *faith* , and one takes this for
truth, another that , and a third de-
nies both , *for many men many minds,*

Jer. 2. 28.
Jer. 11. 13
who multiplie their *faiths* , as *Judah* her *Gods.*

And whilst every one strives to
make good his *opinion* to the prejudice

dice of another, they heap all the *contumelies and reproaches*, upon their adverfary they can devife, and for want of better *Arguments*, will *difparage* his *Doctrine* by *difgracing* his *perfon*; this is the ufual courfe men take when they *divide* themfelves from the *truth*, and want *Reafon* and *Scripture* to fupport their *error*: and no marvail though their foul mouthes be opened againft the *Orthodox*, (whom like Beagles they purfue with opon cry) when they open their mouthes againft God, his *cafe* is the fame with Gods; becaufe God and he maintain the fame *caufe*; and therfore the Pfalmift prai'd, *Arife O God, plead thine own caufe, remember how the foolifh man reproaches thee daily.* Who knowes not that *Herefies* make men infolent, proud and ftubborn, fpeaking perverfe things to draw Difciples after them, by whom the way of *truth* is

Pfa. 74. 22

evil

evil spoken of. It hath ever been the fate of *truth* to meet with oppofition, (*veritas odium*) am I become your enemy becaufe I tell you the truth , faith our Apoftle , truth is faln in the ftreet, and Chrift when he cometh fhall he find *faith* upon earth? many falfe *faiths* , but true faith is but *one*.

Ifa. 59.14.

It is a fure rule, to fet up a multitude of *Gods*, is to deftroy the *true one*; for he is not if he be not *one*, *Faith* is, as *God* is, but *one*, yet although it be *unica*, it is to be lamented it fhould be *fola*.

Great contention there is on all hands, fome for the *truth* , and fome againft it ; yet there is none fo far carried away with a liking of *error*, but pretends *truth*, they fo cloak and conceal their error, that there may be a fhew , fome appearance and probabilities of truth, their doctrine is the *doctrine of Devils*, and therefore

fore had need of *sophistication* to make it either *plausible or passible.*

For lying in wait to deceive, all their engines are set on work, to work men to a belief of that which is false. They speak lies in hypocrisie (saith the Apostle). Knowing that the simple never put it to the *question,* swallows all, takes upon trust, and with *Salomons fool* believeth every word.

2 Thes. 2. 11

Pro. 14. 15.

And some that would be accounted *wise,* (whether for private interest, or personal ingagements, or what other particular concernment I enquire not) are infatuated with the spirit of *error:* for not receiving the *love* of the *truth,* that they might be *saved.*

God sends them strong *delusion,* that they should believe a *lie;* they doat on *error,* and will be miserable in despight of pity. VVe read in Saint *Austin,* in the first of his me-

2 Thes. 2. 11.

ditations

P

Quam ve-
hementi &
acri do'o-
re indigna-
bar mani-
chæis, &
miserebar
eos rursus,
quod illa
sacramenta
& illa me-
dicamenta
rejicerent
& insani es-
sent adver-
sus Antido-
tumqua sa-
ni esse po-
tuissent.

ditations, what he speaketh of the
Manichies raging against the Sacraments, in this case the *Meekneß* of one
side must cure the *madnes* of the
other.

Could they erre with *sobriety*,
keep themselves within the bounds
of *moderation*; and be ready to lay
aside their *error*, when they are con-
vinc'd of it, somewhat might be said
in favour of them; but when that
which with great *peremptorinesse* they
have *rashly* taken up, with much *per-*
tinacie and stubbornnesse they will *ob-*
stinately maintain, and desperately
with bitternesse *flie in the faces* of
such as contradict them, admo-
nish them, or would reduce them;
when by their indefatigable and unwearied wiles they *corrupt* and *ensnare*
the minds of the *simple*; and compasse
sea and land to make a *Proselite*; it is
high time that such be dealt with, as
Seducers, and destroyers of silly souls.

To-

Towards unruly and vain talkers and deceivers, Saint *Paul* directeth *Titus* how to behave himself, *to rebuke them sharply*; and in the *Acts* Saint *Luke* tells us how Saint *Paul* handled *Elimas* the Sorcerer; for he that is an Heretick, if he will not be *reclaimed*, must be *rejected*; when they become intolerable, cast them off; if they will not be brought to the unity of the faith, but desperately seek to destroy it, and seduce men from the right way, they are enemies to *meeknesse*: whom no fair means can reclaim, *rigour* and extremest severity is fittest for them: this for *Seducers*.

Tit. 1. 10.
Acts 13. 10

Tit. 3. 10.

But such as are seduced through *weaknesse* or ignorance, must be pitied, not insulted over: in this way to be profitable, is to be pleasing.

Anger and indignation must be suppreſt, Meeknesse *and* Charity must shine forth, *tears* in the eyes, *grief*

in

in the heart, *compassion* in the bow-els, *tendernesse* of affections must wit-nesse the desire to help them out of their *errour*. *Brethren, if any of you do erre from the truth, and one con-vert him, let him know that he that converts a sinner from the errour of his way, shall save a soul from death.* Overcome them with kind-nesse, though they have erred from the truth in great measure, bring them back, and shut not that Gate of Grace against them, which God hath set open for all; nor with precipitate hast, *be not righteous overmuch*; Is he a *persecutor* of the truth ? such was Saint *Paul* : an *idolater*, an *adul-terer*? *such were some of you.*

    Deal in *meeknesse* with him, and if he fail in *judgment* only, be not too rigid in judging such failings, if from infirmity.

    It were harsh to condemn every *error* for *heresie*, about *truths* of les-

James 5. 19,20

P 2   ser

fer moment, and remote from the *foundation*; all that diſſent from us, or think otherwiſe than we do, are not to paſſe under ſo hard a *cenſure*. It cannot be expected in a world of ſuch variety of men and minds, that all ſhould agree in all points, and therefore let the modeſty of the *Apoſtle* in this *caſe* be our *rule, if in any thing ye be otherwiſe minded, God ſhall reveal this unto you.* Phil. 3. 15, 16.

Better *inſtruction* from *good men,* and further *revelation* from a *gracious God,* may bring them into the *right way,* who for the preſent are in the *wrong.* Beſides, *truths* (we know) as they are not all of one *ſize,* ſo are they not all *revealed* at one time, *later times* have manifeſted ſome *truths* which formerly were infolded in *generalities;* which being throughly ſcanned, a more full, diſtinct, and expreſſe knowledge is attain'd : and unto ſuch to whom they are ſtill *veiled,*

P 3   if

if they come not up in every particular to our *sense*, they are with
meeknesse gently to be entreated, not
rashly to be reprehended ; so many
as build upon the same foundation,
though the superstructure differ.

The *fiery trial* shall manifest every *mans work*, of what sort it is, and
according to his *work* shall his *reward*
be ; let us not therefore *judge* one
another any more ; when God sees
his time, he will *judge* uprightly ; and
then, if we would stand before God
with comfort: let us be sure our *work*
be *good*, our *doctrine sound*, and labour for an *unity of faith*, which until
we can have, we can never have *quiet*. *United in affection* we cannot be so
long as we are *divided in our faith*,
be *one* there, and a *calme* will quickly
follow.

The next, we must labour for an
unity of order, that of *faith* respect-
eth *Doctrine*, this of *Order*, *Discipline;*

pline; the *Doctrine* of *Faith* is upheld and maintain'd by *Order* of *Discipline*, and what *Order* can there be, where there is not *unity*? but where all decently and in a feemely order are united under one Difcipline, there will be quiet; the Apoftle doth often tell us, the Church is but one *Body*, confifting of many *members*, fo diftinguifhed for their *ufes and offices*, yet fo compacted for their *places and order*, that there might be no *fchifm* in the body; for where *fchifm* and faction is, there will be *animofities*, which many times rifes to a greater height, to *biting and devouring one another.* The Church without *order*, is as a *monftrous* body without *fhape*, or as the firft *Chaos*, without *forme*, a rueful *fpectacle*, a *burden* to it felf, and a *prey* to others. Now Unity ever attends Order, and thefe are followed with *meeknefs* and tranquillity, but where *diforder* is,

P 4 there

Gal. 5. 15
Monftrum horrendum informe, &c. Virg. Æneid 3. *Chaos rudis indigeftaque moles.* Ovid. Met. 1. Pythagoras *duo fuprema prin-*

*t'pia conſtituit numerorum : finitum alterum, quod eſt unitas, al-
terum infinitum qui eſt binarius; alterum bonorum, alterum malorum principium. Vnitatis enim natura ſi aeri inſit, bonam
temperiem : ſi animo virtutem : ſi corpori ſanitatem, ſi civitatibus
& familiis, pacem & concordiam præſtat, &c.* Plut. moral. lib.
de Homero.

<table>
<tr><td>

*ἀκαταϛα-
σίας.*
Lyranus,
Hieron.
Tremel.
Tertul.
Oecumen
Eſtius.
Bib.Reg.
*ἣ ἐκκλεσία
ἐκ ἀ'ταξί-
ας ἀλλ
'ἀταξίας
ὁτι διδασ-
καλϑον.*
Conſtit.
Apoſt. lib.
8. cap. 31.
</td><td>

there is *diviſion*, there's *confuſion*,
there's *diſſention*, there is *tumult*,
great *diſturbance*, and things turn'd
up-ſide down; for ſo that word of
Saint *Paul* is by ſeveral Authors thus
variouſly renderd: by which we are
given to underſtand the beauty of
order and unity, which God in a ſpe-
cial manner is pleas'd to own, as very
much conducing to the peace and
quietneſſe of the *Church*, without
which there is nothing but jarres, and
broiles, and rents, heart-burnings,
and ſpleene againſt one another, to
the decay and overthrow of *meek-
neſſe*, which by *order* and *unity* is
brought in, upheld, and maintain'd.
But there are not a few that *ſay* (for
what ends I will not, I cannot ſay)
that
</td></tr>
</table>

that the *beſt way* to peace and quietneſſe, is to give every man leave to ſerve God *as he will*. *How dangerous and deſtructive* this is to *Chriſtian Religion*, let Saint *Paul* ſpeak, for where there are *ſchiſms*, (and *one* ſerves God in this *faſhion, another* in that, and a *third* in a forme differing from both; where there is this *diverſity of worſhip*, diviſion about Diſcipline, take heed of *corruption in Doctrine*) Hereſies are not farre off.

How great an enemy to peace and quietneſſe, and conſequently to *meekneſſe*, let experience ſpeak; our enemies could wiſh no greater *miſchief* amongſt us, than to ſet us at *oddes*, where we ſhould be moſt at *one* (in the worſhip of God) *hoc Ithacus velit, & magno mercentur Atridæ.*

Quamobrem quicunque vel ſublatam diſciplinam cupiunt, vel ejus impediunt reſtitutionem, ſive hoc faciant data opera ſive per incogitantiam, Eccleſiæ certe extremam diſſipationem quærunt; quid enim futurum eſt ut unicuiq; liceat quod libuerit. Calv. Inſt. lib. 4. cap. 12. para. 1.

λέγω κỳ δ̀ιαμαρτύρομαι ὅτι τὰ εἰς ἄιρησιν ἐμπεσεῖν τὸ τ̀ω ἐκκλησίαν ỏι̃σαι ὀκ ἔλαττον ὅτι κακὸν. Chryſoſt. *in* Eph. *hom.* 11.

Quantarum rixa:um futura ſit carum rerum confuſio, ſi prout cuiq; libitum ſit, mutare liceat quæ ad communem ſtatum pertinent? Calv. Inſt. lib. 4. cap. 11. parag. 31.

In

In the worfhip of God *Liberty* may not be granted to men to do what they will, for if it fhould, what *confufion* would it bring into the *pub-lick* worfhip of God? and God is not the author of *confufion*, but of peace, as in all the *Churches* of the Saints. And feeing I am fallen upon this point, which rightly ftated and refolved, would much conduce to the prefervation of *meeknesse*, let it not feeme an impertinent *digreffion* if I take leave not largely to difcource upon it, but briefly to touch it.

The *Queftion* is not about things that are of abfolute neceffity, things that are *fimply good*, which may not be *omitted*; nor *fimply evil*, which by no means may be *admitted*; for as no man hath liberty to refufe the *doing* of that which is *fimply good*, when it is in his *power*.

So no man hath *power* to impofe
that

that which is *simply evil*, when it is in his *will*.

If in the *worship of God* I be commanded to do that which is *simply evil*, I may withdraw my self with modesty, and make profession, that it is better to obey *God* than *man*.

The *Question* then is about things of *a middle nature*, such as we call *indifferent*, and are left to our *liberty*, which *liberty* about things *indifferent*, we are wondrous apt to *abuse* ; and therefore there is required a great deal of godly discretion in the *use* of it, which must be with all *sobriety*, and *without offence*; not making it an occasion to the flesh to the breach of *Christian charity*, which Saint *Paul* forbids. Gal. 5.13.

Nor a cloak of maliciousnesse to the contempt of a *lawful authority*, which Saint *Peter* dislikes. 1 Pet. 2. 16

These *two* in the judgment of these *two* great Apostles should regulate our

our *Chriſtian liberty* about things indifferent. It is well men know their
liberty, but not fit alwayes to uſe it ;
not at all to be inſiſted on; to the
breach of *Chriſtian charity*, or to the
contempt of a *lawful authority*.

The *nature* and *uſe* of that which
is *indifferent*, are two diſtinct things :
It is not the intervening of either
of theſe (*Authority* or *Charity*) that
can alter or change the nature of that
which is *indifferent*, which ſtil remains
the ſame in the *judgment and conſcience*, free and arbitrary.: but only de-
termines the uſe, and ſo it becomes
to that particular (to whom it is ſo
determined) *neceſſary*.

For that which in it ſelf, and of
its own nature was *determinable* to either part, and ſo left free to the party concern'd to do or not to do it :
upon the acceſſe of a *moral, or legal
injunction*, (by the rule of *honeſty* or
juſtice, the party concern'd is oblig'd.

to

to one part, according to the rule, or precept *negative* or *affirmative*.

Let the *instance* be matter of *order* in the external *worſhip of God*; which order ſuppoſe to be reckoned amongſt things *indifferent*, and ſtill *arbitrary* and undetermined : whilſt it ſo remains, *one* may not *condemn* another, for uſing ſuch or ſuch an *order*; nor is the other to be *cenſured* for forbearing the uſe : but deal in *meekneſſe* one with another ; and every one pleaſe his *neighbour* for his good unto *edification*.

But whilſt either *party* will pleaſe themſelves, they *provoke* one another, and *incenſe* one another : they *judge* one another, and *deſpiſe* one another ; and *grow ſo hot*, that they caſt off all *meekneſſe*, and *burn in anger*, and break out into *contention* one againſt another.

Herein both *parties* are too blame; the *one* in finding fault, and being offended

fended at that which they pretend they can, but ſoundly cannot prove to be unlawful by the *Word of God* ; judging uncharitably of their brethren, cenſuring them for *ſuperſtitious* for doing ſuch things, which upon *falſe grounds* they condemn as *unlawful*. "The misperſwaſion of the un-
" lawfulneſſe of a thing is no obli-
" gation to bind to abſtain from it.

The *other* when they impoſe or require the doing of that by others, which as yet remains *undetermined:* and are apt to fall foul upon every one that joyns not with them in their *practice* (whereas anothers *practice* about things indifferent cannot *determine me.*)

Seeing there is the ſame *liberty* left to one to abſtain, as there is to the other to *act*, in this caſe *let every man be fully perſwaded in his own mind*; and let us all behave our ſelves in all *meekneſſe*, with diſcretion, not unſeaſonably,

Rom.14, 5

bly, or diſorderly, not lightly, or raſhly out of due *time* and *place*, doing our ſelves, or preſſing others to do ſuch actions, which as yet remain *undetermined*; but rather follow after the things that make for peace, and things wherewith one may edifie another.

If what is to be done be *lawful*: if there be not in Scripture any command, or counſel, or example to contradict it (if yet it be not *expedient*) it may not be done though *lawful*: for what is in it ſelf, and in a general reſpect *lawful*, may not be *lawful* (*hic & nunc*;) for the time, and the place, and perſons with whom we converſe doth vary the caſe much.

Men are not to follow their own impetuous wills in *doing* at all times to the utmoſt of that *they may do*: a diſcreet Chriſtian will ſuſpend for a time the doing of that (which is lawful and allowed, and which he *may do*)

do) when it is found to be inconveni-
ent.   The *publick good* should controul the fancies of a *private humour*:
that Christians should be humo ists,
Saint *Paul* dislikes; Christ pleased

Rom 15.3. not himself, nor should we, *left our
good be evil spoken of.*

Believers should behave them-
Col. 4 5. selves so *warily* towards them which
are *without, that they may be won by
their honest conversation;* and therefore the Apostle forbids to give any
offence either to the *Jew*, or to the
Gentile, or to the Church of Christ.

It is to me, and should be to any
man a thing *indifferent* whether many
things be *done* or not *done*; provided
that *offence* be not given by the doing
of them to my *neighbour*, nor *exception* taken for leaving them undone by
the *Magistrate.*

For as *Christian charity* forbids a
man to give just cause of *offence* to his
neighbour.

So

So the *conscience of his obedience*
should be a strong restraint from
breaking the laws and ordinances of
the *Magistrate* civil or ecclesiastical,
who hath power to determine of
Christian liberty, and to judg and ap-
point what *orders* are most decent in
the *external worship* of God.

In matters of this *nature* the
Churches of God according to the example of the Apostles, have ever taken upon them by vertue of that
rule prescribed by the Apostle, to
command all things to be done *decently and in order* : and to see that
things so commanded be duely observ'd. For were it left *arbitrary* to
every man to do what himself listeth
in the external worship of God, nothing would be more *absurd and unreasonable*. And if every society of
men be distinguished by their *several
Rights and Customs*, all being united
in one civil policy, for the mainte-

Q nance

*Hoc primum
habeamus
si in omni
hom'n'm
societate
necessariam
esse politi-*

am aliquam videmus, quæ ad alendam communem pacem, &
retinendam concordiam valeat si in rebus agendis vigere sem-
per aliquem ritum, quem non respui publicæ honestatis interest,
atq; adeo humanitatis ipsius. Id in ecclesiis presertim observan-
dum esse, quæ cum bene composita rerum omnium constitutio e
optime sustinentur, tum vero sine concordia nullæ sunt prorsus.
Calvin. *lib. 4.* Inst. *cap. 10. de externis mediis, &c. parag. 27.*

nance of their *common peace* and pre-
serving of *amity.* If in mannaging
civil affaires, men ever obferve fome
order, which cannot be avoided as
confifting with common *honefty* and
humanity, and every action is *naked*
that is not *clad* with due *circumftan-*
ces, fhould vve think *diforder* and
confufion to be priviledg'd in the *holy*
congregation, which is not permitted
in any *civil Affembly?* grant this and
how *deformed* will the face of *publick*
Religion appear.

And therefore becaufe amongft
men there are fuch diverfity of *man-*
ners,

At quum
in hominum
moribus
tanta insit diverfitas, tanta in judiciis ingeniisque pugna neque
politia ulla, satis firma est nisi certis legibus constituta: nec sine
stata quadam forma servi i ritus quispiam potest. Calvin. Inftit.
lib. 4. cap. 10. parag.

ners, such variety of *minds,* and so great repugnancy in their *Judgments* and dispositions, that no *order or discipline* can keep them in, that is not fenced by some *certain laws:* nor can any *beauty or comeliness* appear in the duties of *Religion* where there is not some *set order* which is by all inviolably to be observ'd.

In this: Men are not to be left to their own *liberty,* to do what they think *fit;* but what the Governors of the *Church* (licenced by supream Authority) shall ordain as *fittest and most convenient.*

For as in every *Church* multitude of unsignificant, and unlawful *Ceremonies* should be declin'd to avoid *superstition:* so it will be very fit (to *avoid confusion and profaneness*) a certain and set form should be us'd, unto which all should be bound that by such means Devotion may be *excited;* and true zeal *kindled;* when we see men go about holy duties with that *Gravity, Reverence, Piety and Modesty,* that betokens the Majesty of God, becomes the dignity of Religion, and concurs with the Celestial impressions in the minds of men.

See Hocker his Ecclesiastical Politie.

Now, *for order and decency!* for ceremonies and circumstances; in the publick duties of *Religion;* our *Lord Jesus Christ in his holy* Gospel hath no where prescribed any *Rule,* nor set down any set form, to which he would have all persons at all times to be necessarily bound. For in his divine wisdom he thought fit to set down Fundamental and Essential *truths* with all things *necessary* to salvation.

Quod ad perfectam bene vivendi regulam pertinebat, id totum complexus est dominus lege sua, &c. Calv. *Inst. lib.* 4. *cap.* 10. *parag.*

But for external *discipline* and *ceremonies* we have nothing from him *specified and expres'd:* because he foresaw them to be *various and changeable* according to the exigencies of times and occasions.

What

What he hath fet down in *general* terms we muſt content our ſelves with, looking to the practice of *primitive Churches,* and to the example of the *Apoſtles* and holy *Fathers* with the *Counſels* (*ſequentes igitur & nos per omnia ſanctorum veſtigia*) their *example* in this caſe is to be our *Rule.*

It is certain in the general, Saint *Paul commands* in the firſt to the *Cor. cap.* 16. at the 14*th.* verſe; and in 14*th.* Chapter of the ſame Epiſtle, at the 40*th.* verſe.

And gives *direction* too about ſome particulars, in the firſt to the *Cor.* the 16*th.* Chapter, at the firſt verſe: and in the 7*th.* Chapter of the ſame Epiſtle, at the 10*th.* verſe; and in the eleventh Chapter of the ſame Epiſtle, and in ſome other places; But not he nor any of the reſt, have taken upon them to ſet down any *form of publick worſhip*

1 Cor. 16. 14

1 Cor. 14. 40.

1Cor.16.1.

1 Cor. 7.

1 Cor. 11,

Q 3   which

which ſhould perpetually bind all perſons. Nor do we find any one of the *Apoſtles* in this caſe peremptorily to command any thing. Indeed we have Saint *Paul* about things indifferent, giving his *advice,* and ſpeaking by way of *Counſel, not Command.*

But neither *Chriſt,* nor *He,* nor any of the *Apoſtles* have peremptorily determined any thing about this matter, Nor preſcribed any particular *Rule,* which all men are inviolably to obſerve, they have only laid down ſome *general Rules,* according to which the *Governors of the Church* are to reſolve particulars: whoſe *diſcretion* with Chriſtian charity, is the beſt Interpreter of thoſe *general Rules* which in the particular circumſtances of Gods *publick worſhip* are to be followed. Now then for the manner of Gods outward worſhip, we are ro ſake our *directions* from the Governors

nors of the Church, whose conſtitutions and ordinances are to be obei'd, not as neceſſary to ſalvation, but accidental, containing not the *ſubſtance of Religion*, but matter of *circumſtance* only, *comly and convenient*, not *neceſſary*; and though not *neceſſary* yet *uſeful*: for all are to *uſe* them: though all do not *need* them: and even thoſe that *need* them not; by the *Rule* of *Charity*, and common *bond* of *obedience*, are *neceſſarily to uſe* them.

It matters not greatly what ſome *contentious perſons* alledge : every man knows how eaſie it is for ſuch as are given to quarrel, to cavil at a *Ceremony*. Saint *Paul* would have ſuch that ſingle out themſelves, to be noted and avoided. For if every *fancy* ſhould be followed, we ſhould be led into ſtrange *mazes*.

In the *body natural* if any vitious humours be obnoxious to the *health*

Quibus tametſi non indigemus omnes tamen omnes utimur quia alii aliis ad fovendam inter nos charitatem, &c. Calv. lib. 4. Inſt. cap. 10 parag. 31.

Q 4   of

of it, a care is taken that by fitting *medicines* they be expel'd: so in the *mystical body*, when any humourists disturb the *peace* and quiet of it, a timely course is to be taken for the *suppressing* of them.

The *weak* are to be borne with, till they may be better informed: but no way to be given to the *wilful*: *Schismaticks* like Sathan seem *modest* in their beginnings, and *content* with a little, but yielding to them in a *little*, doth encourage them to ask a *great deal*, (as the Proverb is) (give them an inch and they will take an ell) for where *impudence* meets with a *yielding nature* it knows no mean; like the *waters* of the *sanctuary*, they rise & grow upon you unmeasurably. First *shallow* to the *Ancles*; straight to the *knees*: anon to the *loines*, and at last to a *river* that could not be passed over.

So let them have their will with the

Ezek. 47. Verse 3, 4, 5.

the *discipline* and they will venture upon the *doctrine*; and if they can cry down the *Ceremonies* , have at the *Sacraments* : for contentious *spirits* know not where to *rest*, till they have *ruind* all.

I will say no more at present to this purpose, but only this : that no *Church* at any time could ever frame a *discipline* so exact, nor ordain *Ceremonies* so innocent, comly and useful that could please all. True it is, *good men* and *godly Christians* will be pleased so long as they see no *hurt*. But *Charity* (youl say) seeks to *satisfie all* : It doth so ! Neverthelesſ if men will not hearken to *reason* ; nor be *satisfied* with that which men of great wisdom and holinesſ, upon grave *advice*, and mature *deliberation*, (following the *steps* of the blesſed *Apostles*, and warranted by the *examples* of the ancient *Fathers*, and continual *practice* of all precedent

(*ages*

Quando nunquam futurum est ut omnibus idem placeat, &c. Calv. Inst. lib. 4. c. 10. parag. 31.

Respice tot doctos viros, & considera quale sit his aliud dicere nec erroris vitcundiam formidare. Cassiod. lib. 5. ep. 3.

ages) have according to the *general Rule* of Gods word determined. If men will be froward, and peeviſh, and wiſe beyond that which is *meet.* If they will take upon them to *ſee* better and further than others, then all that have been before them: how God will approve their *preſumption* I know not.

Quod ſi quis obſtrepat & plus ſapere h'c velit quam oportet, viderit ipſe qua moroſitatem ſuam ratione Dominæ approbet : nobis tamen iſtud Pauli ſatisfacere debet, nos contendendi morem non habere, &c. Calv. Inſt. lib. 4. cap. 11. parag. 31.

Sure I am, their *contention*, all good *Chriſtian men*, and all true *Chriſtian Churches* do diſlike. (ſo S. *Paul*) *If any man liſt to be contentious we have no ſuch cuſtome, neither the Churches of God.* The *Cuſtomes* of the *Church* that conſiſt with *decency, order* and *edification* are to be obſerv'd without *ſcruple or contention.*

1 Cor. 11. 16.

Some are ſo *ſcrupulous, nice* and *waiward, peeviſh and unſatisfied,* that they

they are ever *whining*, they are never pleas'd or content with any *order*,
they *question* all, *doubt of* all, search
for a *knot in a rush*, and dare not go
over a *straw* if it lie in their way, for
fear of *breaking* their shins.

Others are contentious about all
Church orders, censuring all harm-
less *Ceromonies* for *superstitious*,*Popish*,
Antichristian,*Idolatrous*, they clamour
against them, railing and reviling,
although they have all the qualifications requirable in *Ceremonies*, lawful and laudable,) that is to say,

*In numbor few : In substance grave:
In choice descreet : In sight comly : In
observation easie : In signification proper and correspondent :* Which Cere-

Super transversam festucam incedere. Cal *Inst. lib. 3. c. 19.par. 7.*

Proinde modus ut retineatur, illam in numero paucitatem in observatione facilitatem : in significatione dignitatem, &c. Calv. *Inst. lib. 4. cap. 23.par. 14.* Dominus noster Christus Sacramen-

tis numero paucissimis, significatione praestantissimis, observatione
facillimis novi populi societatem colligavit. Ep. 18. ad Ianuari-
um.

* Quod neque contra fidem,neque contra bonos mores,injungitur
observandum. Aug. ep. 118. cap. 2. Calv.ep. ad protectorem An-
gliae 87. Quod ad formulam precum & Rituum Ecclesiasticorum
valde probo, ut certa illa extet a quâ pastoribus in sua functione

discedere

discedere non liceat. Calv. ibid.   Calvin.*ep.* 200. Anglis.Fran-
cofordiens.

*Legitimæ Ceremoniæ Senatu Ecclesiastico institutæ,&c.   Etsi
non per se;tamen lege charitatis observandæ sunt adeo ut qui eas
contemnit, & contumaciter cum scandalo negligit sit reus violati
ordinis & rupti charitatis vinculi coram Deo* Bucan.*loc. Com.*33.
de libertate Christiana, Sect.15.

Zanchius *de externo cultu* quæst. 4.

Pet. Martyr. *in ep.* ad Hooperum.

*In descriptione communionis & quotidianarum precum nihil vi-
deo in libro esse descriptum quod non sit ex divinis literis desump-
tum, si non ad verbum ut Psalmi & lectiones tamen sensu ut Col-
lectæ* Bucer. *ep. Scrip. Anglic. cap.*1.*pag.* 456.   *Religione igitur
summa retinenda erit, & vindicanda hæc Ceremonia. Idem ibid.
Ceremoniæ sunt externa humanæ infirmitatis rudimenta.* Calv.
Inst. lib. 4. *cap.* 10. *parag.* 31.*Talibus adminiculis ad pietatem
excitemur.* Calv. *Inst. lib.* 4. *cap.* 10. *parag.* 28. *Omnino enim
utile illis esse sentio hoc genus Adminiculi.* Ibid. *par.* 24. *Sunt
quidem & nobis hodie externa quædam pietatis exercitia, quibus
ruditas nostra indiget.* Calv. *in* Joh. ver. 4. *Vide* Calv. *in epist.*
379.   *Adiophora quándo præcipiuntur sunt quodam modo neces-
saria,* the Princes imposition and Churches determination
doth cause a kind of necessity. Beza *Ep.*24.

David Paræus in Rom. 14, 15.   * Melanc. *loc. com. de libertate Christiana. Libera est Ecclesia vel retinere hoc genus traditionum, vel abrogare & quicquid communi consensu in hoc genere
statuit Ecclesia, & piorum doctorum authoritas, in eo non est per-
tinaciter resistendum, sic bona conscientia retinemus in ecclesia
certos Ritus ex veteribus, &c. qui vero simpliciter omnia putant
abolenda esse quæ accepimus, non solum per se impia, verum etiam
indifferentia, & per se non mala, cum possint retineri sine peccato, in bono usu & non violata charitate Ecclesiæ consentientis:
ii nihilo sunt meliores, quam illi qui affingunt necessitatem in hoc
genere traditionum servando : sicut enim illi qui contendunt hujusmodi*

u'modi traditiones necessario servandas esse, constringunt consci-
ntias & tollunt libertatem Christianam, ita & isti qui affingunt
necessitatem in iisdem traditionibus abolendis, in eodem sunt vitio,
& inimici libertatis Christianæ sine qua salvari nemo potest.

.(*Melanchthon* hath excellently written to this purpose in his
Common Place of Ceremonies, where he advises juniors to beware that they be not *Phanaticks*, &c,)

Steckelius *Annot. in loc. com. Mel. de liber. Chris. pag.* 125
prope finem.

monies so composed to *decency order*
and *edification*, have the approbation
of the most eminent reformed Di-
vines that lived beyond the seas, as
Calvin, Beza , Bucer, Melanchthon,
Steckelius , Peter Martyr , Zanchius,
Bucanus, Paræus, and others.*

By which it appears what *little rea-*
son there is; there should be *such swel-*
ling against the *practice* and *use* of
things *indifferent,* (the observation of
order and *decency* in the *worship* of
God.) Whereas in all things, *order*
and *decency* is commendable: it comes
from *God,* is seene in every *Creature.*
Look on *Heaven and Earth,* we see
comeliness in their *fabrick;* *order* in
their

their *site ; beauty* in all : without which the World were *Tohu* and *Bohu.*

How much more excellent is it in the *Church,* which is the *Schoole of comelinesse and of order,* and is a name not of *Seperation* and *division,* but of *concord* and *union :* the *Church* is compar'd to a well-ordered *Army;* now an *Army* of all *Assemblies* can least bear *Disorder;* disorder it, and ruine it : by which is intimated unto us, the necessity of *order* in the *Church*

VVhat a *monster* will a *Christian assembly* be, without *order* , let Saint *Bernard** speak: not a *people,* but a *rabble;* a *Babel,* not *Jerusalem;* not a place of *peace* and *order* , but *confusion.*

Schola Decori Clem. Rom.lib.8. cap.31. Τὸ γὸ τῆ ἐκ-κλεσίας ὄ-νομα, ὐ χω-ειστμῦ ἀλ-λα ἐνώσεως ϗ συμφωνι-ας ὅγιν ὄ-νομα *Chryf. Hom.* 1.*in* 1 *ad Cor. Cant* 6.4. 10.

* *Da unum, & populus est, tolle unum & turba est* Eraf. *Paraphr. in* Acts 1. *ubi fine fædere pacis, fine observantia legis, fine Difciplina & Regimine, acephala multitudo congregata fuerit, non populus fed turba vocatur; non est civitas fed confufio; Babylonem exhibet, de Hierufalem nihil habet. Bern. in Ded. Eccl. Serm.* 5.*vol.*2. *pag.*349. D.

the

The *Church*, I have told you, is compar'd to a *body*; a *body* confifts of many *Members* or limbs, thefe by *nerves* or *finews* and *joynts* are knit together, are acted and moved.

* *Calvin* tells us, the *nerves* or *finews* of this *myftical body* are *Difcipline*.

*Quemadmodum falvifica Chrifti Doctrina anima eft

Ecclefiæ, ita illic difciplina pro nervis eft, qua fit ut membra corporis, fuo quodque loco inter fe cohæreant. Calv. Inftit. lib. 4. cap. 12. parag. 1.

Saint *Paul* faith the *joynts* are order and *unity*.

Eph. 4. 16.
Col. 2. 19.

If the finevvs be broken, or if there be a *Contortion*, a *Contraction* or *Convulfion* of them; a *Luxation* (*folutio continui*) a *diflocation* of the Joynts, by which the parts of the body are kept and held in their *Contiguity* and *continuity*; though the *body* may live, it is depriv'd of *action and motion*: at leaft its *motion* is both *uncomely and painfull*. Thus *Schifme* and *Divifion* puts

puts the body out of frame, out of *Joynt* (so Saint *Paul* implies) when noting the *Schismes* in the *Church of Corinth,* he declares they were *disjoynted:* exhorting them to be set *again* or perfectly *joyn'd* together, for so the word imports. To take *Vnity* and *order* from the *Church,* is as much as to take *sinews and joynts* from the *body,* by which it is renderd uncapable of *action,* unable and unfit for *motion*; no limbe is able to help it selfe, or to be *usefull* or serviceable to the *body,* but is a trouble and grief to it selfe, a vexation and torment to the whole body.

This is the present state of this *Church,* it is quite out of *frame,* miserably *disjoynted,* disordered, distracted and dismembered, torn into pitiful *rents* and *Schisms* and *factions,* how bitterly and satyrically doth one inveigh against another, what rude *contentions* and uncivil *contestations*? how

names all about it. One man is *worthier*, another man is *holier*, a third is *wiser*; such they know they are, and such they must be accounted, any the least *abatement* in point of *reputation*, is harsh and unpleasing. *Diotrephes* must 3 John. 9. have the preheminence, he must be honoured before the *people*, and. if the *people* will not do it, he is lifted up in his own conceit, like *Simon Magus*, giving out himself is Acts 8. 9. some great one.

It is not *the truth*, but their *reputation* they labour to maintain, and when they *erre*, they think it a *disparagement* to confesse their *error*, and therefore put themselves to *poor shifts* to maintain it. I will not say but some of these men that think so well of themselves, had some cause so to do, could they have kept themselves within measure, but they must *conjure* up unruly

R 2

ruly *spirits*; who taken with their parts, and for worser ends, help to maintain the *faction*, cry up their *Leaders*, who gotten into the midst of a *croud*, the silly *people* that are carried away with *Hobubs*, (like cattel that follow the steps of those that go before them) for companies sake will bustle, and busie themselves to do they know not, they care not what.

Secondly, beware of *coveteousnesse*, another enemy to *meeknesse*, the *love of money* is the *root* of all *evil*; this is a *furious lust*, and where it is obeyed, it *rages*, *robs* and deprives a man of all *quiet*.

What *quarrels* have been raised in *Church* and *State* about this *golden Ball*? From whence comes envie, strife, railings, evil surmisings, perverse disputings of men of corrupt minds, and destitute of the truth? From whence all this unquiet

1 Tim. 6. 10.

1 Tim. 6. 4, 5.

unquiet ? but from this Satanical delusion (*that Gaine is godlinesse.*) It is *evident*, and he that will not shut his eyes must see it ; That the greedy desire of the *Churches means*, hath *created* unto her, her greatest *troubles.* What scufling is there to keep by *greedy dogges* that can never have *enough*, looking to their own *way*, every one for his *gain* from his *quarter* ; not caring what becomes of *Church* or *State*, so they may thrive, tumble all into a *confusion*, what care they.

Isa. 56. 11.

What *scratching* to get that *morsel* that must again be *vomited* up ? How many men have been ruin'd for no other *cause*, but that they had somewhat to lose ? somewhat that might stop the mouths of devouring *harpies* ? He that is greedy of gain (saith *Solomon*) troubles his own house : but if he be a man in

Prov. 23. 8
Interdum fortuna pro culpa est.
Sen. de Clem. lib. 1. *cap.* 2.

place

place and power, he troubles a whole
Kingdom. He that hasteth to be
rich, cannot be *innocent*; when
mens *desires* are too immoderate, and
too eagerly set upon the *world*; how
unquiet are they in themselves, and
what troubles do they bring upon
others; so, if you would have *meeknesse*, beware of *coveteousnesse*.

Thirdly, Beware of *envie* and
malice, for these are great *enemies*
to *meeknesse*, where these are, there
can be no *quiet*, every one will be
some body; and he that hath no *suf-
ficiencie* to raise himself will make
a *ladder* of any *mischief*. Who can
stand before *Envie*? (saith *Solomon*)
Abel could not, nor *Joseph*, nor *David*, *Moses* and *Aaron* must be brought
down, though the *Conspirators* sinke
to *hell*. What supplanting and un-
dermining, like *Lisander* peecing
out the *Lions skin* with the *Foxes
tail*; what *malicious and envious*
men

Prov 27.4.

ınnot do by *force*, they will
by *fraud*.   What ſtrong
ıs, what deadly *conteſtations*
:viliſh *luſts* have rais'd? let
us ſpeak, what ſlanders, ca-
, and odious aſperſions have
own upon their *competitors*;
n aliqua nocuiſſet mortuus eſ-
ıie and Malice will rake *Hell*
hievous deviſes; and ſuch is
ıre of theſe *paſſions*, whilſt
r others, they *torment* them-
Beware of *Malice* and *Envie*
enemy to *Meekneß*.

thly, Beware of *Ignorance*,
blind enemy, but a *bold*
hborn, *rude*, *boyſterous*, *an un-*
and unteachable humour,
y if it be *affected*: When
ın (ſaith *Solomon*) conten-
ith a *fooliſh man*, whether
or *laugh*; there is no *reſt*.
eare robb'd of her *whelps*
man, rather than a *foole* in
his

Invidia Si-
culi non in-
venere Ty-
ranni Ma-
jus tormen-
tum.

his *folly*. Bray a *foole* in a mortar, use all means, do what you can, say what you will, *He will be*, *He still*.

But such as are not wilfully *ignorant*, but *ignorant* through *weakneß*; time and experience may work them to a better *temper*; if they have erred, their error discovered must be retracted; if they have gone astray, they must yield themselves to be reduc'd. If God do open their eyes, whereas they were blind, let them not be shut against the known truth. Frowardnesse, waiwardnesse, pettish, and peevishnesse, are the individual companions of *ignorance*; it is troublesome to deale with, wherefore if thou wouldest retain *meekneß*, beware of *ignorance*.

Fifthly, Beware of *suspicion*, an enemy also to *meeknesse*.

Men that are conscious to themselves

Pro. 17. 12
Pro. 27. 22.
Cui usus est homiuis errare, nullius nisi insipien tis perse-verare in errore. Ciro Phil. 12 Est enim humanum peccare, sed belluinum in errore persevera-re. Cicero. Orat. in Vatinium.

felves of any *naughtineß*, upon auy occafion are apt to judge others as *naught* as themfelves, efpecially if they fhall perceive *worth* in a perfon they hate, they will labour to *eclipfe* it all they can : will greedily entertain any *fufpition*, and cunningly foment the fame : what will they not *do* that are *bafe*, that others may be *thought* as *bafe* as they; they'l lie, and flander, and fay and do any thing to bring into an *Odium* the man they hate.

. To let go *particulars*, this curfed humour, what *mifchief* hath it not done? what *jealoufies* have been raifed by the wicked *fomentors* of our unnatural diftractions? which fet on work by the *Devil*, what have they not devifed to blaft and blurre the perfons to whom they ftand ill-affected?

This is the ▰▰▰▰▰ of the foul that eats into it, and will eat out all
grace

grace and goodneſſe. It is not *good-neſſe* nor *innocencie* that can privi-ledge a man from *ſuſpition* : yea, the *better* and more *innocent* a man is, the more he ſhall be ſuſpected of wicked men, who if by all their prying they cannot find him faul-ty, they will be ſure by their wick-ed and falſe imputations to make him ſeem ſo.

A good diſpoſition will be ever ready to give *a good conſtruction*, but hatred doth hatch *Cockatrice egs,* and what prodigious *monſters* hath it not *brought forth?* whereas they that have the *fear of God*, will not raſhly *judge* others; but what doth not *malice* and *ſpight* utter againſt the moſt *innocent?* the man is *fault-leſs,* but they are *ſelf-will'd,* nor is *innocence* a ſhelter againſt *evil-tongues, malice* never regards how true any accuſation is, but how *ſpightful.*

Sixthly,

Sixthly, Beware of *Novelty* and *Levity*, great enemies to *meeknesse*; It is a disease that many are sick of our *Epidemical disease*; we are naturally *unconstant* and long for *Novelties*, which no sooner had and enjoy'd, but we grow weary of them, and are only constant in *unconstancie*; that which pleases *to day*, *to morrow* is cast aside, and after some *certain dayes*, with great content resum'd, which yet in the midst of the delight it brings, and in its best liking is *loth'd*.

Look upon *Reuben*, unstable as as water (and read his doome) *he shall not excel*. Wavering men like waves of the sea, whom every *blast of vaine doctrine* doth tosse up and down (*weak as water*) restlesse as wind, no man knows where to have them, altering their opinion (I had almost said Religion) as the Almanack doth the Dominical letter

every

Quod voluit spernit repetit quod nuper omisit. Horat. *Inconstantia fastidit amicos.* Plut. *Mor.* *Aliud stans aliud sedens cogitat.* Saluit. *Orat. in* Cicer.
Gen. 49. 5
James 1. 6

every year; we know what they believe this year, we know not what they will believe the next. Let but an *African gale* blow, sounding some *novelty,* and how quickly are they *puffed up*! The *frothy agitations* of unquiet *heads,* and windy *inventions* of unsetled *brains* do carry them up and down as they please; these mens persons they have in admiration, violently contending for them, and are refractary, obstinate, perverse and wilful; *and like children,* at the sight of some *new toy,* let go all the *gewgayes* in their hands, and there is no quiet untill they be filled with it.

Yea, some like the *Camelion* (which turns it self into every *colour* he cleaves unto, save *red and white*) will be any thing but *just and innocent.*

And would you think it? there are

[marginal note:]
Chamele on mutare totus nec aliud valet, 2am, cum illi coloris prop ie:as una fit, quid accessit inde suffunditur Ter. lib. de Pallio. c. 3. Chameleon colorem reddit semper quemcunq; proxime attigerit prae ter Rubrum candidumque. Plin. natural. hist. l. 8. c. 33. de Chameleon:e.

are that would do by their *Religion* as they do by their *clothes*, change the *fashion* every summer. Not unlike the *Hyæna* that changes his *sex* every year.

Oh how good were it could we shake off our *Novelties*, and follow the *Rules* of reverend, learned, wise, godly and innocent *Antiquity*, that we would not too much doat on the *degenerate child* of our *own fancie*, but modestly submit our selves *to better and abler judgments*, which until we can do, we can never live in *quiet*.

The enemies of *meekneß* (you have heard) are *Pride*, *Coveteousneß*, *Envie*, *Malice*, *Ignorance*, *Suspition and Levity*, which (if we would have *Meekneße*) we must beware of, for these wonderfully *disturb* the heart, and marveilously fill it with *perturbations*. How quickly doth *passion* overcome us? how

stiffe

Hyæna, si annalis est, marem & fæminam alternat. Tert.lib.de Pallio.c. 3. *Bonum est patribus obedire, & detrahere proprias novitates* Justinian. *Ep. Siciliæ ad Petrum* Antioch. *in Concil.* Constinapol. 2.

stiffe are our wills? and how *rest-lesse* and *unquiet* our *affections*? which would not be, would we *put on Meek-nesse.*

We should therefore labour for *Charity, unity, humility; and a good Conscience,* that we may *get* this *Royal Robe* and *weare it,* to the *Glorie* of *God* and *honour* of our Christian *profession.*

That so ! *God* may *own* us and *accept* us, and *make good* his precious *word* unto us.

To guide us in judgment.

To teach us his way.

To beautifie us with salvation.

For he will save all the meek upon earth.

Crowning their dayes with *peace* here, and with *eternal blessednesse* hereafter. *AMEN.*

FINIS.

www.ingramcontent.com/pod-product-compliance
Lightning Source LLC
Chambersburg PA
CBHW030353270326
41926CB00009B/1084